piece by piece

piece by piece

A Life Remembered through Things Lost

KIM DANIELSON

SWP

SHE WRITES PRESS

Published in 2026 by
She Writes Press, an imprint of The Stable Book Group

32 Court Street, Suite 2109
Brooklyn, NY 11201
https://shewritespress.com

Library of Congress Control Number: 2025916867
ISBN: 979-8-89636-058-2
eISBN: 979-8-89636-059-9

Interior designer: Katherine Lloyd, The DESK

Printed in the United States

Names and identifying characteristics have been changed to protect the privacy of certain individuals.

For Calvin, Cooper, and Crosby

"Nothing is ever really lost to us
as long as we remember it."

—*The Golden Road*,
L.M. Montgomery

prologue

I looked everywhere.

For months, I searched pawnshops and consignment stores, watched and read the news with an obsessive regularity, and sent the police any information that might be helpful to the investigation. Neighbors sent me their camera footage, and I scanned every frame for a clue. Hours spent sifting through online posts looking for anything bearing a resemblance produced only a few hopeful look-alikes, but never the real things. I shared the story with friends and strangers, hoping for one conversation or detail that could open a new door or spark an idea. But the leads always fizzled, and eventually, my big news became old news. People forgot, the police lost interest, and everyone moved on to the next thing. There's always a next thing. Although the case failed to move forward, I knew I needed to or at least try another way.

That's when I found the words.

I sat down at my desk and wrote about my stolen belongings. It started with a brief description of every item's origin and meaning. The more I wrote, the more I revisited different times in my life. Old and new memories surfaced. I engaged family members and friends in a series of beautiful conversations that filled in the holes and provided more details and colors. I moved decades' worth of boxes in a dark attic to uncover my hope chest. It turns out hope can be found under a thick layer of dust. We simply might forget to look.

Inside the chest, I found photographs and letters; pouring over them revealed answers to questions I never thought to ask, and might never have asked, had it not been for this unexpected loss. The laminated pages of scrapbooks and albums had yellowed with time, but the information contained within them had survived. I found the words, and the words turned into stories. Stories can survive, but only if we tell them.

chapter 1

January 21, 2022

"What happened to our closet?"

Ted's voice rose over Taylor Swift's indignation as I lifted the phone to my ear. Something in his inflection made me sit up straighter.

"What do you mean?" I reached for the dashboard and turned the volume down so I could hear him better.

"It looks completely ransacked. Clothes everywhere."

Trying to remember if I'd abandoned dirty laundry or discarded outfit choices in the closet before I left the house, I craned my neck to see through the foggy windshield as I waited at the stoplight. It was true that I could create a mess deciding what to wear, but *ransacked* seemed a bit extreme.

"There's a broken drawer on its side here," he added.

"I have no idea what you are talking about."

"Everything is on the ground."

"What do you mean *everything*?" I turned off the music. "Where are the boys? Where's the dog?"

"The boys are here. Buddy is sleeping on his bed. But I—" he stopped.

"What?"

"I see the passports on the ground. It's a mess in here and—"

"Passports?"

I leaned forward, the seatbelt went taut across my chest.

"Is the safe open?" I asked.

"Uh . . . Kim . . . I think . . . uh . . . someone . . . broke in here . . ." My husband, usually straightforward and hurried, stumbled over his words.

"Is the safe open?" I repeated, louder this time.

I knew for certain I'd locked the passports in the safe. A sour taste filled the back of my throat. If they were on the ground, it meant the safe's contents had to be—

"Yes." Ted's voice cut into my thoughts. "The safe door is open. They broke into it."

They.

At that moment *they* entered our lives. Not only our home. Our lives.

"I'm so sorry—" he said.

"Call the police," I interrupted. "Now, please."

I tossed my phone down on the passenger seat with enough force that it flipped and fell to the floor of the car. Lowering my forehead against the steering wheel, I thought, *No. Please, no.*

Someone behind me honked a horn.

I knew the exact contents of that safe. My mom's ring. My grandma's jewelry. My wedding rings. It wasn't even a reliable safe. I'd only bought it as an extra precaution one day in Home Depot because the word *fireproof* on the box made me think of a friend's recent house fire.

Another horn sounded. I blinked and looked up, suddenly aware of my surroundings. The light ahead of me had turned green. Cars moved in both directions outside.

A life can shift in the time it takes for a red light to turn green. An upending can take place in a matter of moments.

I pressed the gas pedal and pulled forward into the intersection, doing my best to drive carefully while my mind raced. I'd put my most valuable things inside that safe and tucked it high on my closet shelf behind a stack of sweaters. I never thought

I'd ever need the safe and the extra step to retrieve its contents had always seemed more annoying than necessary. But I kept it, you know, in case of a fire.

I turned onto the street of Cal's middle school.

There were other things in that closet, too, pieces of jewelry that weren't in the safe. I started mentally cataloging everything I'd stashed in small dishes and boxes on the shelves and inside a nearby dresser drawer.

I'd made it easy for them.

I am the only daughter in my family and the only granddaughter on my dad's side. Throughout my life, without realizing it, I'd become a repository. The jewelry of generations had passed to me. I welcomed it, even if my care was only a guardianship, a waiting room for the next person in line. But now the implausible proved possible. All the beautiful keepsakes entrusted to me for safekeeping were no longer safe.

As I entered the car line that snaked through the school parking lot, I noticed the other drivers, many mothers like me. It made me think of the line of women who had given me jewelry pieces as gifts. Suddenly, I felt as if a curtain descended to divide us. Me on one side, the women of my family on the other, their faces fraught with disappointment over this loss, over me. An unspoken promise, now broken, that I would protect their beautiful things.

"Stop," I said out loud.

The sound of my own voice yanked me out of the spiral. I glanced at my reflection in the rearview mirror. My red eyes stung, and my face appeared to belong to a girl who couldn't find her mother rather than a grown woman who needed to pick up her son.

"Stop," I repeated and wiped some pre-tears away with my finger, not giving them a chance to drop. "Pull yourself together."

I didn't have all the details or information. I knew there was an open safe, a broken drawer, a lot of things on the closet floor, and nothing else. Maybe everything I assumed was gone was still there, hidden under the mess Ted described. And, if people had broken into the house, maybe they were looking for something else, something entirely specific. Or maybe they hadn't been looking for anything at all and just grabbed a few items or some cash. I know I left cash in the drawer. Maybe they just took the cash and overlooked or missed the important things.

Wait, I told myself. *Take a breath and wait until you know for sure.*

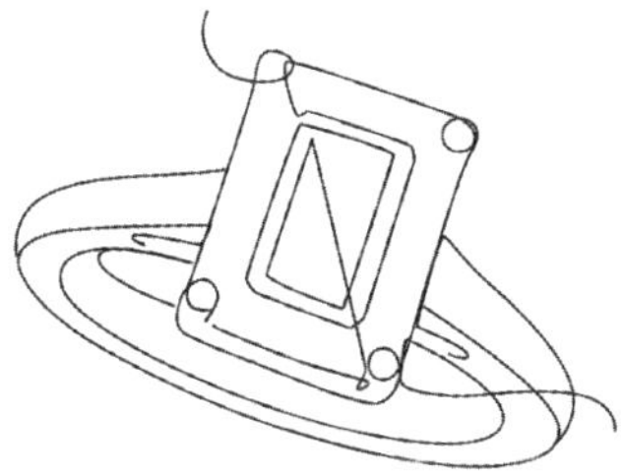

Blue Topaz Ring with a Gold Band

The name "topaz" has different origin theories. Some historians believe it refers to a small island in the Red Sea formerly called Topazios, from the Greek word meaning "to seek" or "to guess" because a thick fog often cloaked the island's shores. Although early writings attribute this island with the production of topaz, evidence suggests it was peridot instead. Other scholars believe the name stems from the Sanskrit word for heat or fire, topas.

Topaz is a hard and durable stone and is often associated with strength and confidence. Ancient Egyptians believed topaz could protect a person against harm. Some people even alleged topaz could make a person invisible. In modern times, topaz is considered helpful in the relief of fears and anxiety.

chapter 2

1994, Littleton, Colorado

We sat around the table after eating slices of yellow cake with white frosting. The *Happy 18th Birthday Kimberly*, originally written in cursive with red icing, now read, *ppy hday rly*, with more than half the cake served onto small plastic plates. Unfolded cloth napkins, crumbs, and plastic forks with icing-coated tines lay scattered on the tablecloth.

My mom handed me a white jewelry box.

"This is from us. We love you."

With a sharp inhale, I lifted the lid. A large emerald-cut blue topaz sparkled inside the velvet-lined crease.

"Wow," I whispered as my eyebrows arched. I looked up to catch my mom's gaze.

She smiled back at me, nodding, as if to say, *Yes, it's really yours.*

I carefully pulled the ring out to examine it more closely. A thin yellow-gold band supported the blue stone, a beautiful shade of blue I'd never seen before in my life. Like the Caribbean Sea, though I would not see that water for another nine years. Like the color of my bridesmaids' dresses, though I would not select them for another eleven. Like the color of my son Cooper's eyes, though I would not meet him for another seventeen.

My mom leaned toward me. "What do you think?"

"It is so beautiful," I said and slid the band onto my right ring finger. "I love it."

I held up my hand and instinctively spread my fingers. Tilting my wrist up and down, I delighted in the sparkle as the kitchen light hit the stone from different angles. I brushed the smooth top of the topaz with my other finger.

My grandpa pushed his eyeglasses up the bridge of his nose. "Kim, let's see," he said, encouraging me to reach my hand toward the center of the table.

Everyone let out a collective "*Oooh.*" Everyone except my two younger brothers, Nick and Adam, both of whom appeared totally unimpressed. Nick tapped his feet under the table and Adam slumped over it, head resting on a bent elbow. They were more than ready to get back to whatever important business my mom dragged them away from for this dinner. "It's your sister's birthday," she had called to them from the bottom of the stairs, until they relented and finally emerged from their rooms, dressed in clothes more appropriate for sleep than dinner. The grown-ups, however, appreciated the moment.

This ring, more than any other gift or event of the day, made me feel like a grown-up. More than the number eighteen displayed on my cake, more than all the birthday cards containing some variation of the phrase *you're an adult now* written in calligraphic fonts. More than the opportunity to vote in the upcoming national election. The milestone birthday hadn't felt like a milestone until I saw that ring on my finger. Before that day, only my mom owned the real jewelry and the beautiful things. With this ring, I owned something real and beautiful too.

Only a fully fledged someone could be trusted with something so important.

•••••

I graduated from high school the following spring and spent the next three months trying to capitalize on time with everyone I loved, as if I were deploying for war across an ocean and leaving home for years, rather than simply going to college in California.

That summer, I worked the same job I'd had every summer since I was fifteen—lifeguarding and coaching the neighborhood swim team. In the evenings, I squeezed in time with friends who also had plans to leave for out-of-state schools. We made the rounds of all things Colorado, like concerts at Red Rocks, movies at the Festival Theater, and late-night hangouts at Daniels Park. But we spent most of the time standing around each other's kitchen islands, laughing and crying about the past and the future, promising to write letters, and swearing to each other that we'd never, ever change. We didn't, and we did.

Throughout the summer, I tried memorizing those moments, afraid that leaving home would mean I'd forget them. One evening, after the sun's harsh rays had settled into a soft and illuminating glow, I parked the car that I shared with Nick by the curb in front of our home and sat in the driver's seat for a moment longer than necessary, staring out the windshield.

One neighbor, still dressed in his work clothes with his tie flipped over his shoulder, squatted in the grass while adjusting a sputtering sprinkler head. Another couple I knew from up the street walked their golden retriever on the sidewalk, the dog zigging and zagging from the grass to the street, switching direction with the clicks of a retractable leash. Two young boys I'd babysat a few times were throwing a football in their front yard. One missed a catch, and the ball flew into the street. The boy stopped and looked both ways before he ran to pick it up, glancing in my direction as he did.

I called hello through my open window. He smiled with a quick wave before scurrying back to his game.

I grabbed my things from the car and got out, leaning my back against the door to stare at my house, the place I'd always think of as my childhood home. My parents planted aspen shoots in the front of the house shortly after we moved there. Now the trees stood taller than the roof. The prominent cement crack in the porch step became ever more obvious, growing with the years as the number of photos we took on it increased and filled more pages of our family albums. I had stood on that porch with my friends in costumes for Halloween and in dresses for Homecoming. From my spot on the street, I glimpsed a portion of my headboard, part of a white wicker set complete with a matching desk and dresser, through the window of my second-story bedroom. I thought of all my hours at that desk, late into the nights, furiously writing about angst in my journals or attempting to memorize the periodic elements for Chemistry class. I probably spent even more hours staring into my dresser mirror with its thick woven frame, willing my frizzy hair to be straighter and meticulously following eye makeup application instructions from *Seventeen* magazine.

I glanced to the right, up the long driveway that curved around toward our garage and thought of my dad cursing the north-facing direction of the house because any snowstorm required hours of shoveling. The backboard lines on the basketball hoop had faded over time in the Colorado sun and snow, but I could still see the unnecessarily competitive games of HORSE (or PIG if we were short on time, and especially if I was winning) with my brothers.

My mom opened the front door, breaking the chain of memories and pulling me into the present.

"Are you okay?" she asked, holding her head tilted to one side with a dishtowel cradled in her hands. She must have seen me through the kitchen window and wondered why I lingered at the car instead of coming inside. "What are you doing out here?"

I smiled. "Just remembering some things."

"Okay then," she said, her tone hesitant. "Dinner's almost ready."

"Coming." I hoisted myself off the door and headed up the front walkway.

I paused for a moment on the porch and stared at that familiar crack. I knelt and ran my finger along it. The cement still radiated warmth from the summer sun. The jagged edge felt gritty underneath my skin, and some flecks of dust broke off and stuck to my fingertip. Even hard things can crack sometimes.

A month later, my parents and I crammed the back of our white Ford Explorer with all the necessities for dorm life such as clothes, scrapbooks, extra-long twin sheets, and the all-important lavender, pop-up handle caboodle to house my toiletries. I secured my topaz ring in its white box in a Ziploc bag that I placed in the niche between the front seat and the folded-down back seat. I wanted it close, at arm's length. We decided my dad would make the long drive with me to California while my mom stayed behind at home with my brothers.

As we left our neighborhood, we drove past the familiar houses of families I'd known since we first moved there. I babysat their kids and watered their plants when they were on vacation. It was the kind of community in which everyone knew each other and people stayed for a long time, a place with deep roots. We passed the neighborhood pool, not yet open for the day. I spent countless hours there as a kid, meeting up with friends to practice diving and perform synchronized swimming routines. That pool also became my workplace as a teenager, the best job with the easiest commute.

We turned onto the main street. "Look at the mountains," I said.

"Pretty amazing," my dad said.

The low early morning sun cast a beautiful orange and purple glow on the mountains in the distance, a gift of a view. As we drove on, I realized how often I had neglected to appreciate it, the kind of realization that so often happens with things when you lose them. At least the mountains weren't going anywhere anytime soon. They'd still be there at Thanksgiving. I promised myself that when I came back home, I'd look at them more often.

We continued our journey, heading west. Soon enough, those mountains would be in the rearview mirror, though it felt like they already were.

I noted all the markers of suburbia at every red light. Grocery stores and fast-food restaurants. Parking lots and neighborhood entrance signs. White papers on streetlamp posts. Missing cats and homeowners association meetings. The roads were lined with trees and fences, beyond them squares of freshly mowed lawns in diagonal tracks. We saw only a few other cars on the road at that early time of day. We didn't speak, matching the silence outside the car, reluctant to disrupt a town just waking up.

A few hours into our I-70 drive we passed by major ski towns like Vail and Aspen. I never took to skiing like I expected I would, like most people would expect anyone from Colorado should. I couldn't bear the cold and had a terrible fear of falling and breaking a leg or an ego.

Wintertime might be popular in my home state, but no landscape beats the Colorado mountains in late summer. We passed a small herd of buffalo at pasture, standing still as statues. On the other side of the road, wildflowers bordered a river rapidly flowing over smooth stones and wayward branches. The highway cut through a deep forest filled with aspen and spruce trees, a stark contrast to the lights, streets, and houses of the suburbs.

It's hard to think why anyone would ever leave a place so beautiful. But then again, I left the mountains for the ocean.

Two days, several gas station stops, a few cheap meals, and one shady Utah desert motel experience later, my dad and I pulled up to the University of San Diego campus. When he put the car in park and turned off the ignition, the anticipation that had been building for over a thousand miles catalyzed into reality. My stomach churned.

"I'm not sure I can do this," I murmured. My inner voice began her monologue, directing how I should react, despite what I felt. *Be excited*, the voice told me. *Don't be nervous. Everyone else is nervous too.*

"Well, we're here. It'll be okay. Let's go check it out," my dad said with his usual upbeat encouragement. And I knew, after fifteen hours in the car, there was no way we were going to turn back.

A student host with a bright blue t-shirt that read AMBASSADOR on the front greeted us with a cheery "Welcome" and pointed the way to my dorm. My dad and I each grabbed a few items and began the haul. Within minutes of stepping inside the building, I felt the furthest thing from welcomed. A glance at the students scrambling around me immediately signaled I did not fit in with this California crowd. My Birkenstocks and cargo shorts made a stark contrast to what I saw in those halls. I instantly noticed the dress code memo that I missed: style, brand names, and exposed skin.

My roommates had arrived earlier. We all stood together with our parents in a cramped room intended for two, rather than three, occupants. Instead of two single beds, we had bunkbeds and one single. My people-pleasing instinct kicked in, and I offered to take the top bunk as a gesture of friendship and a display of benevolence. No one objected.

After I slid some of their hanging clothes over on the closet rod to make space for my own, I stood there, my back to everyone in the room. *I don't think I belong here*, I thought. *I want to go back home. I'm not ready for this.*

I squeezed my eyes shut to fight back the tears, reopening them to stare at the closet wall. Dad, behind me, recounted the traffic at the California border.

Come on. I shook my head to jostle my thoughts. *Stop. Pull yourself together. This is normal, this is the way things are supposed to go. Everybody feels this way after leaving home. You've been here less than an hour. Give it a chance. Give them a chance. You don't know anything yet.*

I dabbed the corner of my eyes with the bottom of my shirt, spun around, and stepped forward into the conversation with a smile, determined to be unaffected by something so silly as my distinctively unfashionable clothes or as childish as a little homesickness.

Two days later, I called my mom in hysterics.

"Mom, my clothes are all wrong." Sniff sniff. "Everyone here wears dresses. Every day. Dresses, dresses, dresses." Sniff sniff. "Why didn't I bring dresses? Why don't I have any dresses?" I sighed deeply.

"I'm sorry," she said. "Tell me more."

"I don't fit in here. I can't see myself in anyone here. They look beautiful and fancy, like they're from another world. I think they might be laughing at me behind my back."

She listened. She didn't try to make me see my irrationality or diminish my very real desire for belonging. She didn't tell me that standing out is better than fitting in or to stop worrying about what other people think. She hung up the phone and headed to the mall.

The very next day, I received an overnight FedEx package from home at the campus mailroom. I ripped the seal of the yellow bubble mailer at the counter as soon as the clerk handed it to me. Pops of bright colors and various floral prints spilled out of the top of the envelope.

Dresses.

My mom knew how to fix things, to make things better. Especially dresses. In ninth grade, I mustered up the courage to ask a boy to a Sadie Hawkins-style dance at my all-girls high school. We found the perfect dress—dark green velvet, knee-length, off-the-shoulder, and a scallop trim around the top. In those years, my triangle of frizzy blonde hair extended to my chin. It would take time and the discovery of life-changing hair styling products for the frizz to find its way to curls. But for this dance, and the duration of high school, the pyramid look remained intact. Luckily, earlier that afternoon, my mom took me to the Macy's counter for a makeup session that helped me look the part of a John Hughes heroine.

Proud of my transformation, I steeled my nerves until the walk out to the car, when I stepped forward and the tiny slit in the back of the dress split, tearing and shooting up a few more inches, dangerously approaching the underwear zone.

Sweat sunk into the velvet. Nothing about my hair or makeup mattered at that point. Instead, my focus centered on whether I'd be walking into that dance with a backless dress, an outlandish choice in the 1990s era of bagginess. The scalloped trim already revealed nude shoulders, so an aggressive slit up the back of the dress would have been way too revealing and a catastrophe of epic proportions.

"We got this," my mom said. "Don't worry. I can fix it."

And she did. With a combination of duct tape, needle, and thread, she mended my dress and most of my nerves. She was good at mending things. She was good at making things okay.

•••••

Thanks to my mom's quick thinking (and quick shopping), I felt more at ease and decided to try and settle into California life.

My roommates, Anne (from San Francisco) and Stacie (from Los Angeles) proved essential allies. They introduced me to In-N-Out Burger and real Mexican food (neither of which were very conducive to the new clothes, but that was before I really cared about such things). We talked late into the nights about all the important topics (boys, almost exclusively boys) and somehow figured out how to share one landline phone attached to the wall in a tiny room with no privacy. Anne and Stacie both knew other people at school, so I could glom onto their party invites as well as their bravery to go. Anna and Julie had a room across the hall. Ellen lived a few doors down from them. By October, I had enough people who cared to make my first birthday away from home feel special.

I fell in love with my literature classes and survived my math classes. Only in California would a professor take his students outside to discuss Shakespeare under palm trees. I spent a lot of time in the library because my dorm room offered no space or quiet for studying, even on the top bunk. The shared bathroom down the hall took a few weeks and a few times forgetting a toothbrush or a towel and having to go back to the room to get it, but eventually I figured out the routine. Thank goodness for the caboodle.

I had friends and good grades, both of which gave me enough strength and confidence to carve out a little life for myself.

But I still missed home. Swaths of nostalgia swept over me at random and often inopportune times like in the middle of conversations or classes, and certainly in the middle of the night. Eyes open and staring at the ceiling (a very close ceiling on that top bunk), memories and images played in my mind like a flipbook on its way to animation.

I'd picture the aspen trees and white wicker furniture. I'd imagine my parents sitting at opposite ends of the kitchen table during dinner. My dad always used a dishtowel as a napkin and draped it over one knee. My mom, always alert for bad posture and table manners, promised we'd thank her one day for the reminders. I'd see my friends in their oversized sweatshirts stretched out on our living room floor as we quizzed each other for history class and discussed what we were going to wear for a dance. I even missed the shoving battles with my brothers in the back of the minivan. From a distance, even the hard memories turned sweet.

Everyone experiences homesickness during their first year of college. That's what they told me would happen. Expect it. It's normal. You'll get through it. But I didn't expect the deep melancholy that accompanied it. That didn't feel normal and often it didn't feel like something I'd get through. I had the sensation of floating adrift and felt lonely without being alone. I would have called it anxiety if I had the word for it back then.

One night I stood inside a deli marketplace on campus called "the Del." It took me a year to be able to say *the Del* out loud without cringing but eventually the SoCal culture abbreviations began to stick.

The Gin Blossoms sang through the speaker in the ceiling above me. The smell of coffee grinds and baked bread wafted in the air. Ceiling light panels illuminated the shelves of food in a florescent glow. People moved around me at a frenzied pace, and I caught bits and pieces of conversations. A few phrases, a few names, a few laughs.

"Remember when he—"

"I could not stop screaming!"

"Where did Steph say she'd meet us?"

Someone bumped into my shoulder.

"Sorry," I murmured reflexively, turning to see that the person didn't even notice me. Unfazed by our collision, he kept his pace and strode out the door. I felt invisible, but maybe that's what I wanted to be in that moment.

The air around me vibrated with excitement, but I couldn't catch onto it. Instead, I felt another one of those aches for home. I needed to walk, or cry, but I found both options impossible. Instead, my hands started instinctively kneading into each other as I stared at the checkered tile floor.

Why should I be so sad? I'm only standing in a deli on a Tuesday.

As I squeezed my hands, I caught the edge of my ring and looked down at it. Every time I saw that blue topaz, I saw it as I did the first time my mom gave it to me. With my left thumb, I traced the flat rectangle.

I thought of my mom at home, over a thousand miles away, and imagined her sitting on the couch watching an episode of *Law and Order* with my dad. Or maybe at one of the stools at our kitchen counter grading fourth-grade tests, her hair tucked behind her ears, and turquoise reading glasses perched at the end of her nose. I glided my finger across the top of the stone and wondered if she thought of me at that same moment. I bet she did.

She told me she missed me every time I talked to her on the phone in my dorm room, my feet dangling over the side of my bed and the phone cord stretched across the room like a clothesline. We talked almost every day, conversations that generally involved tears (mine) and good counsel (hers). She reminded me things would be okay, even though things would change.

But I missed her. That hadn't changed.

I slid the ring up and down my finger, feeling how it caught every time I passed it over my knuckle, and thought about the day I left for college.

Mom stood at the top of the driveway, and I clung to her, laid my cheek onto her shoulder the same way I did as a baby, as a sick toddler, and as a broken-hearted teenager. There she was, that little girl inside of me who never fully grew up and who hated saying goodbye to her mom.

We didn't exchange any words, only that last long hug. When it came time to leave, I walked away from her, opened the passenger car door, and slid into the seat. My dad reversed the car, and I watched my mom, still standing at the top of the driveway. She took a few steps forward, toward us, but we continued reversing away from her. Streaks of blonde in her auburn hair caught the morning sun and glistened to match the dancing aspen tree leaves behind her. She raised one hand to wave and lifted the other to wipe tears on her cheeks. I saw her lips mouth the words *I love you*, and I whispered the same under my breath, watching her reflection in the side mirror until we made a turn, and she was gone.

My childhood memories overflowed with scenes that included my mom, but this one stood out from the others, probably because it was a goodbye.

Years later, I'd look back on it as the first goodbye.

I heard her voice in my head.

"I love you," she said. "Everything's going to be okay."

I opened my eyes and stared at the ring.

"Can I help you?" the man behind the cash register asked me.

It took me a beat to recognize the present moment again. I glanced down, noting the same black square tile underneath my two feet. People milled around me. I raised my gaze to meet his eyes.

"No," I said. "But it's okay. I'm okay."

The clerk tilted his head in confusion and stared back at me.

"I'll be okay," I said more confidently, glancing down at the ring. I slid my hand into my pocket, took a few steps backward, and walked away.

chapter 3

January 21, 2022

At school, I exited the car line for an open parking spot in front. After turning off the ignition, I reached across for the phone I'd tossed after hanging up with Ted, unbuckling my seatbelt to stretch across the console before grabbing it with outstretched fingers.

Tapping on Ted's number to make an outgoing call, I counted in my head and waited for him to pick up.

Ring. Ring.

The dashboard clock read 3:12 p.m. It had only been four minutes since I hung up with him. How is that possible, I wondered.

Ring. Ring.

"You've reached the voicemail . . ."

No answer. Good. Hopefully, he was talking to the police. I clicked to end the call and dropped the phone into my lap.

You're here to pick up your kid, I reminded myself while staring at the school and trying desperately to stay in the present. But the brick building blurred as condensation turned to ice at the edges of the windshield. I thought back on my day, recalling the last few hours, and replaying what had happened that afternoon in sequence, trying to determine when and how a break-in could have occurred.

It'd snowed that morning, so I'd shoveled the driveway before

I'd left. Every time it snowed, I thought of my dad and cursed our north-facing house, threatening an icy danger zone if I neglected it and drove over the snow instead. Across the street, the neighbor's front yard had taunted me in the sun. I envied their walkway, already half-visible, and the remaining snow softening by the minute. After shoveling a portion of the driveway half-heartedly, I'd decided to stop and save the rest for later. I had lunch plans that day, and I never had lunch plans. I didn't want to be late or keep my friend waiting. Dress boots and flimsy gloves were hardly appropriate for the task, but I'd moved just enough snow to back up the car on clear ground. Good enough. I set the shovel on the side of the house, vowing to resume my work on the driveway when I returned.

That had to be when the break-in happened. The realization brought me back to the present.

I quickly texted Cal: *Hurry out. We have an emergency.*

Reaching for the key, I turned the engine back on. My fingers were stiff, and I started shaking from the chilly cold air outside trying to force its way inside.

I rubbed my hands in front of the heat vent and peered through the windshield, scanning the entrance of the school, and willing the building doors to burst open and the first wave of kids to exit.

"Come on, Cal," I muttered. "Hurry."

Counting the seconds, I felt a small relief as the first kids started filing out, their backpacks and coats a sea of bright colors, jostling and bumping each other as they ran to the bus or the cars waiting for them. Then I finally spotted Cal's blond hair. He broke from the pack, bounding toward me. He hopped up and swung both of his legs over a fence, crossed the field in a sprint to my car, and opened the door.

"What happened?" he asked, taking long and heavy breaths as he climbed in and shoved his backpack to the floor.

"Everybody's okay," I managed to say the words with relative calm considering my internal chaos. "Just get your seatbelt on, and we'll go."

I pulled out of the lot.

"Mom," he said, pressing harder for an explanation.

"We think someone broke into our house this afternoon." I tried to keep my voice as level as possible.

"What? What do you mean?" he asked with alarm. I sensed his blue eyes fixed on my profile, reading my face for clues.

"We don't know anything for sure." I didn't want him to think the world was ending, but I couldn't lie either. "Dad called a few minutes ago. He thinks some people broke in and went through our things. They ransacked our closet."

There's the *They* again.

"Are Cooper and Crosby there? Is Buddy okay?" he asked, trying to wrap his twelve-year-old mind around the information and, of course, worrying about the dog as much as his siblings.

"Everybody's okay. Dad is there with the boys. No one was home when it happened except Buddy, and he's fine. He probably slept through the entire thing, the big lug." I forced a lighthearted tone.

Cal exhaled. "That's good." He turned and looked out the window.

That is good.

It was good. He was right.

The boys are good. The dog is good. We are all good.

Isn't that what matters?

Of course, it's all that matters.

Try to keep some perspective, I told myself. *Keep focusing on what is important. Everybody's okay.*

Cal turned back toward me. "What did they steal?"

"I don't know yet. But I'm worried they took Mimi's ring

and other important things because Dad said the closet was a mess and the safe was open."

"What did you have in the safe?"

"Mostly jewelry. My wedding rings. Some important things that belonged to Mimi and Grandma and Granny, things I was hoping to maybe pass down some day, things that remind me of them. Heirloom stuff. Just stuff, but important stuff to me." I rambled on, trying to explain it to myself as much as to him.

Cal considered my words in silence for a moment. "Well," he said thoughtfully, "maybe they didn't take everything."

"Yes. Maybe they didn't. That's what I'm hoping. We just need to get home and see for ourselves. Dad isn't answering his phone, so I hope the police are there with him now."

"Did they go in my room?"

"I don't think so. But I'm not sure. I haven't been home yet. We'll see when we get there."

"Okay," he said, resigned.

"Everybody is okay," I repeated, for both of us.

Traffic moved at a snail's pace, and no matter how many times I weaved or changed lanes, even taking a side street to try to get home quickly, I hit every red light on the route and pulled behind every slow driver on the road. We both stayed quiet, and I kept trying to clamp down on my feelings so Cal did not notice or take them on himself.

But as soon as we turned into our neighborhood, I felt my insides seize again. Especially when I saw a police car parked in front of the house.

Please God, I silently prayed. *Please let this not be what I think it is going to be.*

I pulled into our driveway with more speed than I should have. We both jumped out of the car as soon as I turned off the ignition and silenced the rumbling engine.

A dread settled over me as I grabbed the handle of the door to the house. I wanted to know, but I also didn't want to know. I wanted to stay in this moment of hope where "Maybe they didn't take everything." But I knew I couldn't. So I took a deep breath, and on the exhale, I pushed the door open and went inside.

Platinum Necklace with a Diamond Pendant

Heirloom: something of special value handed down from one generation to another through family members.

The word "heirloom" originally referred to a piece of property considered part of a family estate and subject to inheritance laws. By the twentieth century, however, the use and meaning of the word expanded beyond the law to family custom and now commonly refers to personal keepsakes of meaningful importance that have belonged to a family for generations.

chapter 4

2002, Boulder, Colorado

Cloaked in my black graduation robe with a poofy tam on my head, I walked with my classmates from the law school to a lecture hall on the main quad for our graduation ceremony. Family members lined the streets of the University of Colorado campus and clapped as we made our way down the final two-tenths of a mile stretch of a long three-year marathon. My parents, brothers, grandparents, and aunt cheered as the dean read my name and handed me my diploma. The bar exam still loomed ahead in a few months, so I wasn't officially out of the woods with outlines and all-day study sessions, but graduation certainly merited a celebration.

I met my family for lunch at one of my favorite restaurants in Boulder. Glasses clinked and voices competed for airtime above the harsh screech of chairs scraping across the floor as people scooted in and out of their seats. The clamor rose higher than usual on that day, as it surely did in all college-town restaurants during graduation week.

"Any interest in dessert?" the server asked as he cleared our plates.

I considered ordering another glass of wine but worried it might send me straight into an afternoon nap and implicate the party plans that were lined up well through the night. I opted for coffee instead. Nick ordered some chocolate explosion dish, and my grandpa asked for a slice of cheesecake. Adam asked about flavors of ice cream. I leaned back into the booth, the combination of the wine and the morning events rendered a lovely buzz that I didn't want to fade, at least not yet.

My dad reached across the table and placed a black box with a red bow in front of me. My mom handed me a card. "Open the gift first," she said.

I untied the bow and lifted the lid. My eyes widened, and I looked up at my parents.

"What is this?"

I held up a long, shimmering necklace and draped it over one hand. A circular pendant encasing a solitaire diamond dangled at the bottom of the chain. The contemporary half-bezel setting bracketed the stone and made the diamond appear as if it had broken through the platinum disc. I had never seen a piece of jewelry like it, so modern and delicate; it reminded me of a piece of art. The metal flashed in the light under the table's dangling pendant lamp.

"Now the card," my mom said.

I slid my finger under the envelope's overlapped triangle, breaking the seal, and pulled out a letter.

Dear Kim,

As you begin this new journey in your life, we wanted to give you something special to keep with you. In 1972, we bought this diamond as we decided to start our lives together.

We had hopes and dreams of getting married, raising our children, and growing old together. Never, in any of our dreams, could we have imagined how perfect things would turn out. Thirty years later, we love each other even more—and have the most wonderful family we could have ever imagined.

Today, we get to be with our beautiful daughter as she graduates from law school. We are so proud of you! We are proud not only of the remarkable things you have accomplished but also of who you have become. You have grown into a beautiful, generous, and loving person. We are so fortunate to have you as our daughter.

Now, on this special day, we want you to have this diamond as a reminder of our love for you. Our hope is that thirty years from now, you will feel as proud, fortunate, and thankful as we do today.

We love you,

Mom and Dad

Her expectant gaze met my eyes as the significance of this gift slowly settled over me.

"I don't know what to say," I whispered, staring at the sparkling diamond resting in the palm of my hand.

"We are so proud of you," my dad said.

"Thank you." My voice cracked. "This is so beautiful."

Mom reached over as I lifted my hair, and she helped clasp the necklace around my neck. Nothing had ever been passed down to me before that day. I reached up and held the pendant between my fingers.

This is her diamond, I thought. The one my dad gave her when he proposed. I imagined my mom holding out her hand and showing her friends the ring as they fawned over it.

I'd seen several photos of my parents' wedding day: June 14, 1974. My mom wore a white dress with embroidered lace flowers. Her long crimson hair cascaded down underneath her veil and rested atop the stark white of the bodice. My dad wore a baby-blue tuxedo with black trim and more ruffles than his bride. The bridesmaids wore long blue floral dresses and large-brimmed floppy hats, while the groomsmen's tuxedos matched my dad's blue but didn't have as many ruffles.

I imagined my parents exchanging their vows at the altar of St. George's Church in St. Louis, this diamond on my mom's finger as she said, "I do." For better or worse, in sickness or in health, until death do they part.

Now that same diamond hung around my neck, a link to not only my mother but to a time that predated me—a touchstone to the past.

My parents trusted me with this heirloom.

I sat there in the restaurant booth, staring at the stone, considering all of it. Their dreams. Their last thirty years. My dreams. My last three years. An old diamond in a modern setting. A reflection of the past but a hope for the future. Theirs. Mine. Their love for each other now extended to love for me. All in this one stone that carried a big story.

They had passed this important baton to me, which meant they counted on me to protect this heirloom, this forever connection to them. This diamond represented their legacy, and their trust in me as the designated keeper.

chapter 5

January 21, 2022

Inside the house, I came through the kitchen and saw Ted talking to a police officer in the backyard. I considered checking in with them, but my urge to see the closet for myself superseded everything else. I dropped my purse on the table and beelined to my bedroom. Cal followed, right on my heels.

Chunks and slivers of the black sliding glass doorframe littered the bedroom floor. The nightstand drawers and doors were wide open, their contents spilled onto the ground. When I reached the closet doorway, I flinched. Almost exactly what I imagined but worse because I no longer had to imagine it.

"Oh no, Mom. This is bad," Cal said, unable to pretend it wasn't.

I took in the scene. The shelves that lined the walls of the small walk-in closet, usually stacked with neatly organized folded clothes (Ted's more neatly organized than mine) and baskets containing socks and accessories, had been wiped bare. Things lay scattered all over the hardwood floor, discarded like trash.

"I'm really sorry, Mom." Cal backed out of the closet, sensing I needed to be alone and probably wanting to run and check on his own room.

I took a step inside, searching for a spot to place my feet without stepping on something. It reminded me of crossing a river, trying not to lose my balance by gripping the edges of rocks with my toes. With a foot, I nudged some of my clothes to the side to create an open space to crouch down. The tiny space felt frigid, even though I still had my puffer coat zipped and my scarf wrapped twice around my neck. I squeezed my eyes shut.

God, please let this be a bad dream.

But it wasn't, of course, and when I opened them, the disarray looked more alarming, as if someone had put my belongings into an enormous Tupperware container, sealed the lid shut, shaken it, and then dumped everything on the ground. I put a hand on one of the shelves for support. Jewelry pouches were turned inside out, boxes overturned, and baskets emptied. Pajamas and underwear were flung in different directions. I checked the critical things first—my wedding rings, my grandmother's jewelry, and my mom's ring. Gone. I looked at the shelf where I had a necklace tree and tiny dishes of stud earrings. Gone. All the shelves had been cleared. They hadn't overlooked or missed a thing. I thought of that remote possibility of twenty minutes earlier—the hope that they missed some things. That possibility, also gone.

"I can't believe this," I said to the piles around me. But the piles said nothing in return.

I let this happen. I kept all these things in one place, making it so effortless for them. I should have bought a better safe and insisted on an alarm. This was all my fault.

I cursed myself for being so lazy, so sloppy, and so irresponsible.

Sitting back on my heels, I felt the disappointment in my bones. My mother and grandmothers trusted me, and I felt like I let them down. I let my brothers down, my kids, my nephews, and all the next in line, who would never see the treasured heirlooms intended for them.

Voices in the kitchen jolted me out of my self-loathing. Ted and the police officer must have come back inside the house. I shook my head to try and silence the running chatter inside it, forcing myself to stand up and go find them.

The officer stood next to the kitchen island with a pocket steno notepad in his hand. Ted sat at the table. They both looked up at me as I walked into the room. I saw the defeat in Ted's eyes before I reached him. The officer introduced himself and handed over a business card. Ted stood up and hugged me.

"Sorry," he said with a deep sigh. I'd hear that word again and again and again.

The officer followed, "I'll need to see your ID, please," in the same tone he would have used if this had been a traffic stop situation instead.

I stepped to the purse I had thrown on the counter and fished my driver's license from my wallet.

He took it from me, laid it down on the table, and started writing information onto his notepad. He kept looking back and forth from his notepad to my license and from my license to his notepad. He moved so slowly. Too slowly. Like an inchworm. My anxiety started making me squirm. His energy, compared to mine, made me question whether he'd actually seen the closet.

"What are we doing?" I asked, with a volume that bordered on inappropriate. "Shouldn't you be out looking for these guys right now? They're getting away! They're probably at pawn shops trying to sell our things as we speak! Can't you get this information later? We're losing time!"

My harried demeanor ran circles around the officer's calm and cool one. He started into a speech about procedure.

"Are you going to dust for fingerprints?" I interrupted, uninterested in procedure.

"Well, my partner's shift starts in fifteen minutes, and he has the fingerprint kit in his car. When he gets here, he'll do that."

Fifteen minutes, I thought. They could be well on their way across the state in fifteen minutes.

He looked down and continued writing something on his notepad. The walkie-talkie radio clipped to his breast pocket loudly sputtered words, codes, calls from the station, or communications between officers. He reached up and pressed a red button to silence the sounds every few seconds, but the noise and voices over the speaker had the exigency this kitchen conversation lacked.

Shut it off, I thought as I gritted my teeth and glared at Ted, trying to get him to read my mind. Ted caught my eye with a look that said *What can we do?*

He's right, I thought. *Take a breath. Calm down. The police are here to help.*

We followed him back to our room. Ted sat at the end of the bed while I stood and shifted back and forth on my feet. The officer kept talking until a second police officer appeared in the bedroom.

"I told them we would go ahead and do fingerprints," said the first. "I think the kit is in your car."

This is taking too long, I thought repeatedly, looking at one and then the other, glaring with an urge for them to be more efficient. Everyone is too casual for this very real crime scene.

The second officer went back out to his car and returned to the bedroom a few minutes later. He set a plastic box on one of the tables next to the wall. It reminded me of the chemical kit we used when I worked as a lifeguard during high school summers. The box had a hinged top with several different test tube bottles inside. He handled the kit clumsily, knocking it over a few times, which only added to my angst.

I continued pacing back and forth while Ted calmly sat on the edge of the bed, leaning forward with elbows on his knees. A few times, I mumbled to him in a low voice or mouthed it without sound, "What are they doing?" He shrugged every time with an "I don't know."

What can we do?

The police dusted a few things for prints: the safe, a couple of jewelry boxes, and the bedroom door. They took a few photographs with their cell phones. The first officer made a list of contact names in his notebook—neighbors, people who had been in our house recently, and our general contractor who had completed a remodel a few months earlier. They explained what would happen over the next few days but made no promises. They repeated their promise of *no promises* a few more times.

"Burglaries are tough to solve. Your things are probably out of the state by now," said the officer.

Burglaries are tough to solve? Seriously? Are we already giving up solving this crime before we've even tried?

"Out of state?" I asked.

"Yes, what generally happens is that they immediately separate what is valuable and worthless, dismantle parts of the valuable pieces such as stones, and send the valuable things out of state so none of it can be tracked. All the worthless items—they trash. It's close to impossible to trace or locate things when it comes to jewelry or any items without unique identifiers like the kind computers or credit cards have, which makes them easy to track."

"You think it's all gone? It's only been a few hours."

"We can't say anything for certain now, but that's usually the pattern."

I stared at the ground. Anger at my inefficacy began taking root.

The officer lowered his voice and stepped toward me. "Don't lose hope. There is still a chance we can find these people. Or that your stuff will turn up."

I gave him a faint smile. It had been some time since I smiled.

"Don't lose hope," I whispered his words to myself.

Gold Chain Necklace with a Butterfly Charm Adorned with Six Small Diamonds in a Vertical Row

The butterfly develops in a transformation process called metamorphosis, a series of changes that occur over the butterfly's lifespan. An adult butterfly first begins as a tiny egg. A monarch butterfly egg is the size of a pinhead. The eggs hatch in various timeframes, from days to weeks.

Next comes the larva, or caterpillar, stage. The caterpillar emerges from the egg and begins eating and growing. As it does, it splits and sheds its skin four or five times. Some caterpillars grow to one hundred times their size.

After the caterpillar is fully grown, it stops eating and forms a chrysalis, hiding itself under a branch or leaves, sometimes underground. This stage lasts a few weeks to years, depending on the species. During this phase, the caterpillar's body breaks down, and new parts develop, including wings, eyes, and legs.

In the last stage of metamorphosis, the fully developed adult splits the pupal case open, crawls out, and hangs upside down to stretch and dry its wings, a process that takes up to two hours. The butterfly then flies off to find a mate, and the cycle begins again. The female flies and lays her eggs on a plant. The average adult lifespan is two weeks, but it can range from several days to many months.

For some butterfly species, this life cycle can occur in geographic locations vastly apart. The monarch butterfly can fly hundreds, sometimes even thousands, of miles from where it emerged from the chrysalis to lay its eggs. The butterfly's metamorphosis is a symbol of new beginnings and transformation. Many people believe that when a butterfly lands on someone, it can be a sign that something is about to shift.

chapter 6

1981, St. Louis, Missouri

We gathered around the oblong dining table in my grandparents' house. I was five years old. Outside, the heavy and sticky heat offered a suffocation typical of any August day in St. Louis. Inside, the air conditioner whirred loudly and helped us forget it. I crowded close to my mom's chair at the table and watched with a front-row view as she opened gifts for her twenty-ninth birthday.

My grandma's angel food cake, covered on the outside with Cool Whip and sliced strawberries, sat in the middle of the table. My grandpa leaned back in his chair and sipped black coffee, while my grandma, who allegedly had the opposite head seat but rarely ever sat down, bustled around us, moving back and forth from the kitchen, setting down plates with slices of cake and sides of vanilla ice cream. My dad sat in the chair next to my mom, his head tilted toward her with eagerness as she picked up a box that had been expertly gift-wrapped from a store and fastened with a premade bow.

My younger brother Nick flailed on my mom's lap, and she tightly encircled her arms around him, as if holding a big beach ball. She lifted the lid on the box and sighed when she saw the contents.

"Oh Mike, it's so beautiful," she said, pulling out a necklace. I craned over her arm to get a better look. The thin gold chain caught the light from the low-hanging chandelier above the table. We all murmured in excitement as she held the necklace up in the air for us to see. A one-inch golden butterfly charm danced at the bottom of the chain. The butterfly did not hang from a tiny jump ring like other necklace pendants. Instead, the chain was attached to the butterfly's wings. Six small diamonds formed a vertical row down its body, which jutted out from the plane of the wings, giving it more dimension. When she held it up to show everyone, the butterfly dangled in the air right at my eye level, like a real butterfly might flutter past me.

My dad kissed her on the cheek and said, "Happy Birthday, Nancy."

She gathered her hair over to one side and handed the necklace up to him. He gently held the chain with both hands and clasped it around the nape of her neck. The golden butterfly glimmered against the backdrop of her pale, freckled skin. Her off-the-shoulder floral dress allowed the butterfly enough space to shine. I stared up at my mom in awe. She looked like a movie star.

Of all my mom's beautiful things, this butterfly necklace stood out as one of the most sacred to me because I see her wearing it in so many memories. I traced the voyage of that butterfly in the same way I traced the path of my childhood, darting in and out of moments with her in the same way a butterfly flutters from plant to plant.

Decades later, after she got sick, the butterfly landed in a mahogany jewelry box she kept on her bedroom dresser, tucked away in a corner, until a cold February afternoon in 2016. I was thirty-nine years old. Mom was gone, and I was left in charge of her things. I stared at the jewelry box for a few moments before gingerly lifting it with both hands and bringing it over to the bed. The box creaked as I opened the lid.

The inside mirror had yellowed with time. I took the corner of my sleeve and wiped away a layer of dust until a vague reflection stared back at me. I imagined my mom's reflection in that mirror over the years as she tried on different earrings or leaned in close to better see a necklace or bracelet clasp.

Sifting through the various pieces inside the box, I spotted the butterfly nestled in the back, pulled it out with one of my fingers, and held the chain up in the air. The butterfly still looked like it was flying. The gold had a tinge of rust, but it still sparkled in the light that stretched from the window across the room.

Seeing that dangling butterfly immediately brought me back to my grandparents' dining room as I stood close to my mom, in awe of the necklace and of her. I undid the chain clasp and fastened it around my neck. I stepped to the side and looked in the mirror. The wings lay flat on my chest in the same way they did on hers. I closed my eyes, covered the charm with my hand, and remembered. No one would have understood how prophetic that butterfly became when my mom received the necklace and how many changes were ahead for our family.

My parents grew up within blocks of each other in Affton, Missouri, a suburb of St. Louis. Although my dad was three years older than my mom, their families belonged to the same Catholic parish, and they, along with their siblings, attended the parish's school from kindergarten through eighth grade. They had never officially met each other during that time, despite their educational and geographical overlap. They generally knew of each other's families, but any chance for connection diverged when they attended different high schools, as is the all-encompassing nature of high school.

Although they grew up as neighbors, they didn't cross paths until my dad literally crossed my mom's path in front of her sorority house at Southeast Missouri State. She spotted him from her bedroom window as he walked across the lawn and thought to herself, *I'm going to marry that guy someday*. Something about him stood out to her, but she couldn't pinpoint it.

Although the prophecy ultimately came true, she first had to meet that man, and it happened the following summer at a local bar called Fridays. They started talking, and it didn't take long to realize how well they knew each other without knowing each other. They had so many concentric circles that they skimmed right through that initial discovery phase. A story of romantic comedy gold: two people who grew up within a mile of each other and knew many of the same people yet never connected until years later.

A similar serendipity would unfold in my own life a few decades later. But that's another story.

In my parents' case, one conversation led to a date, and that date led to more. One day, my dad proposed, my mom said yes, and they married and entered their next phase together.

First, they lived in a single-bedroom apartment in Affton. My dad worked for an insurance company, and my mom began her teaching career at a local elementary school. I was born in 1976, Nick followed in 1979, and Adam arrived the day after Christmas in 1982. We settled into our first family home in Manchester, another suburb of St. Louis.

"The Westbrook years were the best times of my life," my mom told me. "You kids were young, and I lived close to everyone I loved. Family. Friends. We did everything together."

My mom and her two sisters, who both had kids close in age to us, created a makeshift co-op. We spent time under the watch of my aunts and in basements and backyards with my cousins. Aunt Jan was tight with naps, and Aunt Wendy was loose with television.

Birthdays and holidays were marked by crowded rooms, scampering kids, and tables stacked with Pyrex dishes. Extended family events didn't really exist because everyone came to every family event. Cousins were like siblings, aunts and uncles like parents, and in-laws like blood relatives. Both of my parents grew up this way, surrounded by generations of families, and they imagined the same kind of life with their children.

This vision changed when I was eight years old, the year we began our great—and unexpected—western migration, when my dad accepted a job promotion in Overland Park, Kansas. We had to say goodbye to Westbrook's best of times. We stayed in Kansas only eighteen months before my dad received a different promotion, which sent us further west to Denver, Colorado. Eighteen months is too short for any roots to take hold, so saying goodbye was sad but not as hard as the first move.

When we left St. Louis, my mom struggled with being so far away from home.

"I spent so much time around my sisters and the Westbrook neighbors," she told me. "We were a bunch of young moms who helped and loved each other. We huddled together on couches and back patios. We drank and smoked and laughed together. I never felt alone. But then we moved to a new place where I knew no one. I had never lived so far from St. Louis and missed everyone back home. I had never experienced anything different, never expected life to change, and worried that my kids would miss out. The holidays were the hardest."

But my mom never shied away from a challenge, so without the comfort of family and familiarity, she filled in the empty spaces between the scaffolding of our new world with thoughtfulness, creativity, and, most importantly, new traditions. If our family was a gingerbread house, my mom was the icing that held all the graham cracker sheets together.

My parents began their marriage never expecting to leave St. Louis and its baked-in ways of life, yet after our move, they forged their own way to be a family.

Every New Year's Eve, we banged pots and pans with wooden spoons on our front porch, blindly falling for her trick of equating the New York ball drop in the Eastern time zone with midnight in our mountain time zone. We toasted each other and a new year with sparkling cider and late-night cookies at 10 p.m.

We gleefully ate my mom's green eggs for breakfast on St. Patrick's Day and reluctantly stomached her corned beef and cabbage for dinner. Food dye and warm, sour, wilted lettuce—our tribute to our Irish ancestors.

We spent Mother's Day together at the zoo, her pick every year and professed favorite place in the world. "Why do you love the zoo?" I asked her years later. She never expressed any kind of passion for animals.

"Oh, I don't know," she shrugged. "I guess because it's a happy place, and it's all about family. Who has bad memories from the zoo?"

The longest day of my mom's year happened to be our favorite—the sugar spree and free-for-all Halloween culminating in a trick-or-treating rampage. One blessing of attending Catholic school is that November 1, the day after Halloween, is a holy day of obligation, and school is closed. My mom indulged us by allowing us to eat as much candy as we wanted, all day long.

As much candy as we wanted. For a kid, there was no better combination of words. From the minute we woke up in the morning to the minute before we brushed our teeth at bedtime, we took full advantage of this radical freedom. But the freedom ended at the end of the day, and so did our unlimited access to the candy.

Every Christmas Eve, my grandma and grandpa flew out to celebrate the holiday with us. We began with 4:00 p.m. Mass—one of the two church days a year when my mom insisted we dress better than our Sunday best (the other being Easter, of course). We came home from church to light the luminaries—white paper bags with a couple of inches of sand and a tealight candle—along our sidewalk to match every other sidewalk in our neighborhood.

Then we headed to my aunt's house to open some presents and have dinner. Aunt Jenn, my dad's sister and the only member of my extended family that lived in Denver, always hosted a Christmas Eve buffet dinner. Even her food choices—petite quiche, pigs in the blanket, shrimp cocktail—became embedded in our tradition.

On the way home, we *oohed* and *aahed* at the lights and luminaries as we drove around the neighborhood listening to Christmas music favorites. At home, we changed into our pajamas and crowded together on the couch while my grandpa read aloud *'Twas the Night Before Christmas.* My brothers and I slept in one room together, on the floor, and laid awake for hours talking about what Santa might bring.

On Christmas morning, no one could come downstairs until we heard holiday songs playing on the kitchen stereo, my mom's clue that gave us the go-ahead. Before the first chorus of the first song, we blasted down, screaming in excitement, and started in on our presents. The sight of the family room on Christmas morning gave me the same thrill, no matter my age. Something undeniably magical occurred overnight, even if my parents had a hand in it. My mom made breakfast, and we lazed around all day in our pajamas amidst crumpled shards of wrapping paper. We played board games and overloaded on Christmas cookies.

A virtuoso of small touches, my mom had plenty of non-holiday traditions as well. For our birthdays, the honoree decided on the dinner menu. If we had wanted lobster tail or beef Wellington, my mom would have obliged. But I always chose macaroni and cheese, and she made a ridiculous vat of orange noodles on the stove every birthday. It had to be Kraft, nothing homemade or gourmet, and no sides, either. She piled every plate high with a mountain of processed neon pasta. I ran that mac 'n' cheese request all the way to college. Nick classed up his birthday with spaghetti and meatballs, and Adam chose Taco Bell until he wised up as a teenager and asked for steak dinners.

In our school brown bag lunches, she included short notes of encouragement such as *I love you*, *I believe in you*, or *Do something extraordinary today*. On the flip side of these notes, she wrote a vocabulary word and its definition. She asked us to commit the word to memory and try to use it in a sentence at some point during the day. Even on the days I didn't really focus on the word or threw the note away with the rest of my PB&J or bologna sandwich, the word found its way into my vault and, along with all the others, helped form my lifelong love of language.

Some days, when my mom knew she'd still be working when we got home from school, she planned a scavenger hunt for us around the house. We'd come home and find a note on the kitchen counter that sent us sprinting all over for clues until we uncovered the prize—Necco wafers hiding in the oven or a Big League Chew gum package tucked behind a sofa cushion.

All these echoes from the past spoke louder now that she was gone.

I let my hand drop to my side, opened my eyes, and looked around the room. So many reminders of her. Reminders of all the big and small touches, all the ways she worked to make a house a home and five people a family. Reminders were all I had left.

I reached back up to feel the butterfly resting on my chest, to make sure it was still there. Something had changed again. Another phase, this one without her.

I felt a surge within me, a need to protect the necklace now, to protect the memories it represented and stirred up within me—memories of my childhood, memories of my mom.

This one little charm contained such a big vault.

chapter 7

January 21, 2022

"When are you going to have the fingerprint results?" I asked the officer.

"We first need you and Ted to come down and do elimination prints. Then, we send the prints downtown to be entered into the database. It could take a few weeks to process."

"A few weeks?" I asked. "Why so long?"

"A few weeks at the earliest," he said. "The labs are overwhelmed with requests now."

A few weeks might as well be a few years.

"I want to do it as soon as possible. Do you want us to follow you to do that right now?"

"No, it's too late tonight. You can come down this weekend or Monday."

Waiting until Monday morning—as if criminals need weekends off.

"We will be there tomorrow morning," I said definitively, leaving no room for objection.

Ted continued talking to the officers, but I thanked them, excused myself, and walked back to my room.

Standing in the closet's entryway, I wondered again how this could have happened. As it had so many times that day, my imagination supplied the narrative.

They shattered the frame of the sliding door in my bedroom,

came into my room, and opened every drawer and cabinet in sight. They grabbed handfuls of jewelry and poured them into my handbags. Then they emptied the shelves and dug into every box, every pouch, and every envelope they could find; they flipped open lids and overturned baskets. They figured out how to break into our "in case of a fire, but we will probably never have a fire" safe and stole things given to me from the people who mattered most in my life.

I looked down at the pajamas, bras, and underwear on the floor, and the hairs on my arms stood up straight as I imagined these intruders' hands all over them, rifling through my clothes like dogs tearing up dirt. My stomach twisted as I gathered the clothes.

I bet their fingernails had dirt underneath them.

Every surface they touched appeared so filthy to me now.

I stuffed everything into the hamper, closed the lid, stepped back, and stared at the space, disgusted and furious. How dare they come in here, lay their hands on my precious things, and rifle through my intimate possessions! They had no right to step into my life in such a personal way. This is my home. This is my safe place.

As soon as the clothes had been removed, I saw more pieces of discarded jewelry littered on the floor. I let out a heavy sigh as I knelt and started sifting through what they determined unworthy.

They had no idea what these pieces meant to me. They only considered face value. But value is a matter of attribution and meaning is a matter of assignment.

They knew nothing.

Time to start picking things up, I thought. *Piece by piece.*

I created an open space on the floor and spread out all the earrings in the same way I did with the cards for the matching game, Memory, when I was a kid. I grabbed two of the overturned porcelain dishes on the floor. By some miracle, they didn't shatter on impact. I placed the earring pairs into one of the dishes, and the singles into another. After sorting, I picked up the dish of single earrings, not exactly sure what to do with this collection of halves. Trashing them seemed unfair. They had enough trauma for one day.

I started making a mental list of all the stolen items, and as the list grew, my hope—the hope the officer told me not to lose—faded. Jewelry is the perfect souvenir because it's small and easy to store, the perfect memento because it's unique, and the perfect keepsake because it lasts. It's also the perfect thing to steal for identical reasons.

How could I remember everything I had accumulated over time? It never appeared to be a substantial quantity because it fit in a single drawer and on a single shelf. Jewelry is sneaky that way. But I never made an inventory; it all simply traveled with me, and the collection grew as I did. From childhood home to dorm room to apartment after apartment after apartment to house to house to home. With every birthday and Christmas and anniversary and boutique and travel destination and *T.J. Maxx* visit and hand-me-down, and with every loss of someone I loved, the collection grew.

The old pieces had made room for the new. Like memories did.

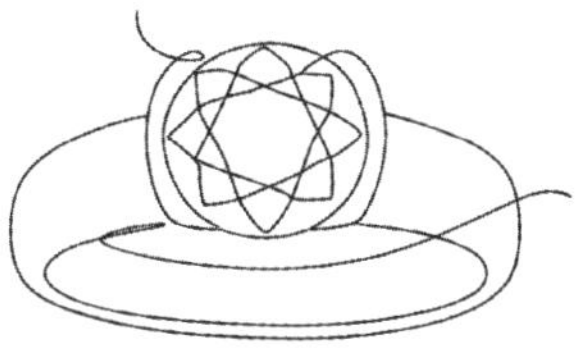

Platinum Ring with a Bezel-set Round Diamond

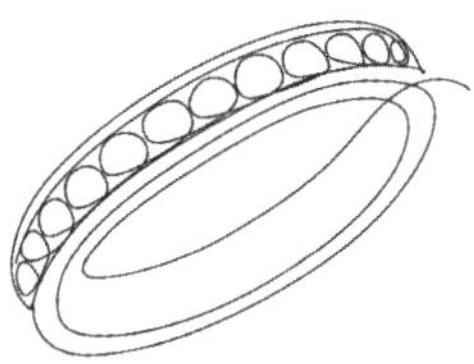

Platinum Eternity Band with Channel-set Diamonds

The origin of the modern wedding band has its roots in ancient Egypt when people would exchange "rings of love" made of reeds or hemp. The circular shape of a ring represented eternity. The Romans continued this practice but with rings of stronger materials such as ivory, bone, copper, or iron. In the second century AD, gold became the standard.

The Romans wore rings to symbolize a contract or love between two people, but the idea of an engagement ring to mark a pending betrothal began in 850 AD. Pope Nicholas I declared rings should be worn as a symbol of a man's intent to marry a woman. Diamond engagement rings, however, did not appear until the fifteenth century when Archduke Maximilian of Austria proposed to Mary of Burgundy with a diamond ring—a stone setting shaped with the letter "M." In the United States, the popularity of diamond engagement and wedding rings grew rapidly, beginning in the 1940s when DeBeers launched its "A Diamond is Forever" campaign.

The placement of the wedding ring on the fourth finger of the left hand also began in ancient times based on a belief that a vein of that specific finger led directly to the heart; this vein was called the vena amoris, *or vein of love. Researchers later debunked this theory, but the tradition stuck.*

chapter 8

2006, Cabo San Lucas, Mexico

Ted and I sat at a table near the pool's edge of the ME Cabo Hotel in Mexico. Even though it had been over a year since our first visit, many of the details were exactly as I remembered. Bistro lights strung around the perimeter swayed gently in the breeze, and tropical house music emanated from hidden speakers in the surrounding palm trees. A few people floated on foam noodles in the water, and others lazed in lounge chairs, sipping frothy drinks with umbrellas. The pool overlooked the beach, with only a few steps down to the sand. We ordered some drinks and relaxed into the oversized cushions.

Even though Cabo San Lucas was a two-hour direct flight from Denver, the airport customs line moved excruciatingly slowly, and the bumper-to-bumper traffic during the car ride to the hotel made it feel as if we had traveled all day. However, the moment after we arrived at the hotel, we quickly changed and headed straight to the pool. Our earlier annoyances disintegrated into the warm air, perfumed with a mixture of saltwater and sunscreen.

The server brought us our drinks—a Corona for him and a salt-rimmed margarita for me. The sun hung low on the horizon like it had decided to sit down on the water and join the party.

Ted did not get down on one knee. That wasn't his style. He simply turned in his chair toward me and said, "I want to spend the rest of my life with you. Will you marry me?" Then he reached into the pocket of his swim trunks and pulled out a ring.

The ring had a thick platinum band and a round diamond center stone secured in a bezel setting, a continuous rim of thin metal appearing like a collar around the stone.

"What?" My eyes widened with shock.

"Will you marry me?" he repeated.

The significance of his words slowly took shape as I repeated them in my head. The proposal came as a total surprise, even though our trip back to this spot and the romantic setting should have clued me into the possibility that something like this could happen. But I'd had no idea.

"Yes," I said. "Of course, I will."

Ted slid the ring onto my finger, and everyone around the pool—who had apparently watched the scene unfold—cheered.

Eighteen months earlier, in the same spot, at the same hotel, with the same ocean view, I never could have imagined such a scene. But then again, I had yet to meet Ted.

In an unusually snowy April, and on a complete whim, my friends Christine, Karen, and I decided we deserved a vacation. One evening, we crowded around Karen's computer and searched for flights and hotels to Mexico. We needed a good deal because the public defender's office where we all worked could hardly be called the most lucrative gig. Luckily, a hotel room with two double beds popped up, advertising a bargain price, and we booked it immediately.

A few weeks later, we packed our bags, stuffing them with swimsuits and flip-flops, and left the chill of Denver for the balmy beach of West Mexico. We arrived at the hotel, changed into our beachwear, and charged straight to the pool, hoping to unwind with drinks in the sun.

At dusk, I woke up face-down in a lounge chair, the lines from the rubber slats imprinted on my left cheek. Christine and Karen were packing up to go back to the room and change for dinner. I fumbled my way behind them. But I didn't make it out again, instead crashing onto one of the double beds, rousing only when the next morning's light peered through the curtain gaps. Apparently, I really needed this break and some sleep. We all did; our jobs required long days, and the work carried heavy implications—the kind that took a toll on body and heart.

We made our way back downstairs and devoured a delicious brunch before settling again into the same row of pool chairs. The relaxing deck music and the surf's sound eroded months of stored tension. Closing my eyes, I drifted into a peaceful doze.

Until a booming voice interrupted it.

Cracking my eyes open behind my sunglasses, I shifted my gaze to identify the source—a man dressed in printed board shorts and a white V-neck T-shirt strutted determinedly aside the pool deck, yelling to another group of men across the pool, close enough to him that he didn't need to yell.

"Hey, do you guys want to go get some breakfast?!" V-neck shouted.

"Where's Stan?" One of the guys in the chair called back to him.

"I don't know—I think he's still in the room!" V-neck hollered again. Does he operate on any other decibel level?

I felt annoyed to be a part of this conversation, but I hardly had a choice. His voice carried, and the familiar pounding in my head returned.

"*Ugggphh. . .*" I whispered to Christine. "What is that guy doing? Why is he so loud? Make it stop."

He didn't stop. Yelling or pacing. I pushed myself up onto my elbows.

"Should I go say something? I don't want to get out of this chair. I don't really want to move. But someone needs to let him know."

But then he disappeared, probably finding whoever or whatever he needed, because the calming music refilled my ears, and I drifted into another vacation half-doze.

By the early afternoon, after a few hours of blissful rest, the sun peaked high in the sky, and the temperature soared. I finally left my chair and crossed the deck to the pool's shallow end to join Christine and Karen on their foam noodles and cool off.

"Be careful, don't get too close," a familiar voice warned me. "My friend just peed in the pool."

I glanced to the side, confirming the voice of the same man who'd been yelling earlier. He sat on the edge, just feet from where I stood. He was quite tan. Possibly *too* tan. Muscles, but nothing overboard. Definitely a fitness guy. A guy who cared that other people knew he was a fitness guy. Anyone could see that. He had a slim face, defined features, and dirty blond hair with some waves. He wore horn-rimmed sunglasses that seemed more appropriate for someone twice his age. I tilted my head to the side, trying to assess whether he was serious or merely seeking attention by making an incredibly juvenile joke. He smiled, and his white teeth reminded me of the snow we had left behind back home. A joke, then.

"Thanks for the heads up," I muttered, rolling my eyes behind my sunglasses, before walking away and wading into the water to sit with my friends at the in-pool bar.

I sat on one of the stools submerged underwater and waited for the bartender to make some frozen concocted slushie drink like a pina colada or daquiri. After a few sips, I noticed the man I'd spoken with join his friends in the water. His group drifted toward ours, and we soon chatted with them.

"So where are you from?" the mystery man asked.

"Denver," I answered.

"Denver? Where in Denver?"

"Do you know Denver?" I still felt somewhat put off by his brusque manner, the yelling, and now this persistent inquiry. "I live in the Baker neighborhood."

"What street?" he asked, shooting me the same pearly grin. "I'm from Denver too. Oh, and I'm Ted, by the way."

"Really? That's crazy." I couldn't help but smile. "I'm Kim."

A few sentences later, we'd discovered that not only did we live close to each other, but we'd also grown up in neighborhoods only a few miles apart in the suburbs. The Denver metro area had grown substantially throughout my lifetime, but everyone who grew up in those neighborhoods tended to know some of the same people and places. Our two-year age difference meant we'd overlapped in high school, which multiplied our connections. Years later, it would occur to me how our first conversation must have mirrored what my parents shared with each other the first time they met. Sometimes, our histories are an echo of a future fate. The door opens, and we walk inside.

The pool conversation led to a walk on the beach, which led to a running race on the beach, where we ran right into a couple of local guys who talked us into renting jet skis.

"What's your last name for this waiver?" Ted asked.

"Intagliata."

"Spelled just like it sounds?"

"Actually, yes!"

"I'm kidding," he grinned. "You're gonna have to spell that for me."

Our full day of making one plan after another turned into plans to meet at a dance club in town. Our two groups converged again, but this time around a single cocktail table as home base. We danced to Maroon 5 songs in a packed bar full of twenty-somethings and whistle-blowing waitresses balancing trays of Jell-O shots.

Christine and Karen left close to midnight, but I stayed out a little longer, not wanting to end the time with Ted. We left the club and returned to the beach, walking and talking along the water's edge. At my hotel door, he kissed me goodnight. There wasn't any question whether I'd see him again the next day; something in my heart told me I would. As I pulled the covers up and sank into the pillows, I heard the drumbeat from the club's music in my ears, a hopeful rhythm.

The next day came as the one before. Our groups met up at the pool. The buzz of elation from the previous night whirred in my head as I grasped for more time with Ted. It seemed he wanted the same, but reality encroached on us. We both had only one more day before we had to leave, return to the cold, and face the lives we'd left behind. I had no idea if I'd ever see him again. We'd made no plans or commitments. Although we had a few indelible moments together, the effects faded even before we left. I couldn't tell if this relationship had real promise—whether it could survive real life. I hoped so, but I had been fooled by false hope enough times to know better.

This was not my first rodeo. I'd had plenty of disappointment when it came to meeting men in bars. I doubted whether it mattered if the bars were inside or outside of a pool, or whether the bars were inside or outside of the United States. As I packed my suitcase to leave, I stopped for a second and sat down on my bed, and texted my friend Jayne back home:

> *Men are no different in Mexico than they are in Denver, especially when they are from Denver and in Mexico.*

As we said goodbye, Ted asked me for my phone number. My expectations had been soured before, so I told him no. If he wanted to find me, he could find me—which sounded more empowered than I really felt. He already knew I worked at the Denver Public Defender's office, and he knew my last name, Intagliata, and even knew how to spell it. We'd established the dozens of people we knew in common. It would not be a difficult task if he decided it was worth the effort. I felt proud of my restraint, standing my ground and knowing that he at least had to put in some work if he wanted to find me.

Of course, I wanted to be found.

Sunburned and tired, my friends and I boarded the airplane and returned to life in Denver. I thought of Ted but never mentioned him out loud to anyone and never with any real belief I'd ever hear from or see him again.

A week or so after our return, an email notification popped up on my screen as I wrapped up a long day of work. One of those mutual friends, Jen, wrote:

> *Ted said he met you in Mexico. He wants to reach out to you. He asked for your number, but I said I'd give you his email address instead.*

I stared at those words on the screen. I had already written Ted off. In dating economics, a week equaled a year. My fingers hovered over the keyboard.

On one hand, I knew we had something special. But on the other, this delay made me suspicious. What had taken him so long to reach out? I sat back in my chair, considering whether to ignore and delete the message. At the very least, I knew I should wait a few days to respond. He had taken his time, so I obviously needed to do the same. That's how the game is played, after all. I weighed my pride against my hope, the risk of potential disappointment against the lure of further connection.

Oh, why not?

Willing my ego to step aside, I copied Ted's email address from my friend's note and wrote him a direct message:

I could have won that race on the beach.

I included my phone number, hit *send*, and sat back in my chair, sighing and feeling a knot in my stomach.

And so, it began.

Ted called me within the hour to make plans for our first "official" date. We would meet for dinner in a few days. Our conversation on the phone only lasted a few minutes, but the easy flow we had in Mexico was missing, like an article of clothing we'd left on the sand and forgotten to pack. The exchange had all the bearings of a blind introduction: stumbling, awkward laughs, and dead air. I worried it confirmed what I feared: the magic wouldn't, couldn't last.

But that all changed when we ran into each other—literally and randomly—the morning of our planned date.

On my usual jog around the local park, I looked up from the well-worn path and saw another runner coming toward me. Ted. We hadn't laid eyes on each other since Mexico. I expected to see him ten hours later that same day, but certainly not mid-jog, early in the morning, in my tatty exercise gear. Seeing my Cabo Ted in my everyday world made me do a double take. I didn't remember that he lived in that neighborhood and ran that same loop daily. How many times, I wondered, had we already run past each other before the trip to Mexico?

That fated run-in—after everything I'd felt for him on vacation—confirmed the opposite of what I'd been telling myself. We had something I needed to pursue; there are only so many coincidences one can blame on chance.

We exchanged a few nervous words, turned on our heels,

and continued our respective runs in opposite directions. I repeated our trail conversation in my head, replaying it over and over on the jog home, wondering what he thought, if I had played it cool, and whether he also saw potential that this could work in real life, that *we* could work in real life.

He must have because he showed up early that night, waiting for me outside in the exact same car my mom drove, even down to the exterior and interior colors. The sight of him in that car made me laugh and totally endeared him to me.

We headed to a new, trendy restaurant with a cryptic name I've long forgotten and a menu boasting its own unique brand of fusion cuisine. Ted and I sat on the floor, cross-legged, cooking raw tuna on hot rocks, laughing at the idea that the chance to cook your own food and pay triple the price while sitting on the ground qualifies a hotspot as hot.

I took a sip of what the server had named "our mixologist's newest and favorite artisanal creation," and didn't ask as much as yell, "What have you been up to since Mexico?" My voice could hardly compete with the roar of the crowd and escalating beats from the sound system, which vibrated the floor and, accordingly, my rear end.

He told me a few things, but most of his answers were lost in the noise, and I couldn't read his lips as the rocks' smoke plume was between us. Our dinner conversation had all the uneasiness of a real first date but also hints of familiarity.

We'd covered a lot of basic Q&A in Mexico, but being back in our hometown, something had shifted that necessitated a reintroduction. We had to make sure we were the same people in Denver that we encountered in Mexico. A few steps backward before we could move forward, together.

Midway through our dinner, one of Ted's friends who happened to be at the same restaurant recognized him and broke into our conversation.

"Hi!" she said, stopping by our "table." Or at least that's what I think she said when I read her lips.

Ted rose to greet her and I followed awkwardly, my legs half-asleep and prickling after being folded so long on the floor.

"This is Kim," Ted introduced us. "She's . . ." He glanced across at me, catching my eye, unsure of how to describe me or even finish the sentence at all.

I knew what he was feeling, this uncharted landscape of ours, and I smiled back at him before reaching out to shake her hand. "I'm Kim."

As the weeks progressed, our connection re-paced, tracking closer to the ordinary course of new relationships. We spoke on the phone most days, made plans for the weekends, and eventually, with time, introduced each other to our friends. I learned how he spent his days, and he knew how I spent mine. Our separate lives merged, and we suddenly planned for months ahead rather than days.

The first time my parents met Ted, we ate dinner at an Italian restaurant called Luigi's. My family had been going there for years; it even shared a parking lot with the movie theater that Ted and I had frequented as kids. I wondered if our families went to all the same movies, if we'd ever been in the theater together, watching the same movie at the same time, this big world so very small.

I waited with my parents outside the front door. Ted came straight from a work event, carrying a hefty gold bowling trophy in his arms like a baby, and immediately presented it to my mom with all the drama of the Olympics.

"Hi. I'm Ted. I brought this for you."

"Wow." My mom laughed. "I've always wanted one of these."

He explained that he'd just finished a team-building bowl-a-thon and had come away the victor. My dad stepped forward and shook Ted's hand. Whatever tension there might have been for this first meeting instantly evaporated. Ted's charm made the awkward stuff easy.

Things seemed off to a good start, for the second time.

I had always gravitated toward the more unassuming and quiet types, the kind of boyfriend who blended in with the background and sometimes struggled in unfamiliar situations, needing pre-game advice on handling my friends and family. But I'd found a person in Ted who was none of those things. He lit up every room he walked into, and his contagious excitement infused the people around him. Ted attracted a crowd everywhere he went, and, just like everyone else, I couldn't resist his magnetic pull.

That's not to say our hard edges didn't butt up against each other. We had our share of disagreements and hurts along the way. Maybe because we had each lived long enough to form opinions and develop our own value systems. Or maybe because we'd each started in our own families, with all those systems in place, and it takes time to forge a new way together.

"You don't believe in the death penalty?" he asked incredulously one day as we walked to meet friends for breakfast. "Why not?"

I stopped and turned toward him. "You do remember I'm a public defender, right?"

"But what if someone killed your best friend or your uncle or . . ."

It wasn't the first time I'd argued the point with another person, but it was the first time we experienced that friction. Ted and I had grown up only a few miles apart, but our experiences with things like politics, faith, and money were worlds apart.

During high school, I wrote letters for the Amnesty International Club, while Ted worked for the student credit union. I went to Catholic school and Mass every Sunday, and Ted grew up without structured religion. After college, he went straight to work and landed a high-paying job in the tech industry within a very short time. When I met him, he owned an actual house with a two-car garage and an en suite bathroom with two sinks. He lived in one of the best neighborhoods in Denver, and his home décor reflected his ability to choose his environment, including orange accent chairs, oversized framed mirrors from Z Gallerie, and legitimate pieces of art.

On the other hand, I carried a hefty burden of graduate school student loans, which my state job could barely cover. I had a monthly lease for the bottom floor of an old house in a "bettering" neighborhood and hand-me-down furniture. My bed didn't even have a headboard, and I'd never heard of the words *thread count*. No house I had ever lived in had a bathroom with two sinks. Growing up, I'd shared a bathroom with two brothers. And instead of hanging art, I tacked photos to corkboards to fill my walls.

Ted took big swings and big risks, while I had always been a rule-follower, scared of getting into trouble and disappointing other people. He showed me it was okay to be unafraid and unapologetic sometimes. Whenever we skied, I always felt more comfortable on the blue intermediate runs, taking big, wide turns to traverse across the entire slope back and forth, slowly and methodically. Ted pointed his skis downhill and went for it, carving quick little turns in the crevasses between gigantic moguls. He loved jumping off cliffs, whereas I'd always opt for the long way down. But we always met at the bottom, and that was how we learned to live together too. Time showed us ways to soften some of those hard edges. We found balance and made our own ways together. It helped that we also managed to fall in love.

Ted designed and chose my engagement ring completely on his own, but we picked out our bands together just a few months before our wedding. One afternoon in July, we went to a local jewelry store, and the salesperson offered us seats in front of a rectangular glass case. Ted spoke with great conviction when asked what we would like to see.

"She wants a ring that is really simple because she's really athletic," he said.

The salesperson glanced at me, and I shook my head and rolled my eyes.

"I'm not *that* athletic," I said with a laugh. "I'd rather have something sparkly, and I can always take it off during these supposed athletics."

When we shifted the conversation to pick out Ted's ring, Ted made another joke that he wanted a band "as thin as possible, so it might blend into my skin."

The salesperson gave me a look that said, "Um, lady, what do I do with this guy?" I shrugged, not explaining how often I asked myself the same question.

What am I going to do with this guy, I thought.

Marry him.

We ended up with two bands: an eternity band with round diamonds, neither simple nor athletic, and a platinum band with a matte finish, neither thin nor skin colored.

2007, Wailea, Maui

We married on a grassy hillside overlooking the ocean. A three-piece orchestra played as I walked down the aisle in a white linen dress with a lace overlay and an ivory orchid lei draped around my neck.

Our family and friends gathered near an enclave of magenta hibiscus flowers. Ted and I held hands and promised to love and honor each other from that day forward.

We took turns sliding the bands onto each other's fingers as a symbol of our commitment to this promise. The officiant blew a conch shell horn, called a *pū,* and we kissed. He closed with a blessing.

I ho'okahi kahi ke aloha.

Be one in love.

After the ceremony, we took photos as the sun slipped away, and at some point during the endless combinations of people, I glanced down at my left hand and caught a glimpse of my wedding band, now paired with my engagement ring. The channel setting of the wedding band protected its own row of smaller diamonds just like the engagement ring's bezel setting protected the diamond center stone. Just like loyalty and love would protect this marriage. I turned the rings around on my finger and watched as they reflected the twilight of the sky.

My mom's engagement diamond—the one my parents had given me in a necklace when I graduated from law school—symbolized their hope when they began their marriage. Now, I had my own wedding rings, my own symbols of hope at the beginning of mine. Time and space unfurled ahead of us to allow for such hope, including the hope that I could one day give these rings to my child or grandchild.

Hope can traverse multiple generations.

chapter 9

January 21, 2022

I heard Ted still speaking with the police officers near the front door, so I walked out to join them. The officers promised to work on the case and be in touch with any developments.

"If you think of any other details, call or email," the first officer said. "You have my information and the reference number on the card. One of us will check in with you early next week."

Next week seemed so far away.

Ted shut the door and turned the lock.

"I don't think we're ever going to see our stuff again," I said.

"I don't think so either."

"I still can't believe this happened."

He squeezed my shoulder. "Yeah, I feel awful about it. I can't imagine how you feel."

Until that moment, I had been so focused on my loss, my things, that I failed to recognize I wasn't the only one who had lost something.

The thieves had stolen three of Ted's watches, which he had planned on giving to our three children. His mom had gifted him one when he graduated from high school. I gave him another watch as a wedding gift. We saved and bought the third together for his fortieth birthday—a vintage pipe dream come true. Ted is not one for sentimentality, but those pieces had meant something to him.

I sighed and shook my head. "I hate this."

"Me too. But let's just focus on the fact that we are all okay. That's the only thing that matters. It could have been way worse."

Ted's modus operandi: Move forward. Don't be sad; be practical. Control what you can control.

My modus operandi: Cry in the closet. Grief needs to be grieved.

But he was right. We were all okay. That was the truth I needed to hold onto with a tight grip.

The doorbell rang as we walked back to the kitchen. I turned, thinking the police had forgotten something, even hoping outlandishly that they already had a lead.

Instead, our friends stood in the window of the door, and the sight of them brought relief after all those anxious hours. Lindsey held pizza boxes in one hand, and Austin held a few pieces of wood in the other for us to use as a temporary repair for our broken bedroom door.

Dinner hadn't even crossed my mind, and routine things like hunger and schedule felt completely arbitrary by that point in the day.

"We are so sorry this happened. We wanted to stop by with some food and to help with the door," Austin said.

"Wow. Thanks," Ted said, taking the pizza. "Really appreciate this. We'll be okay. It's just stuff."

It's just stuff.

That phrase and various versions of it crossed our lips a thousand more times in the days and weeks that followed, though my words had the conviction that my heart did not.

I wrestled with that imbalance. Knowing very well that it was, after all, just stuff. No one should feel sorry for me, and I shouldn't feel sorry for myself. Sure, I'd lost some beautiful things, but others had lost so much more. Jewelry doesn't measure up to *real* loss. Things aren't worthy of grief. It's just stuff.

How could I ignore the obvious privilege that I'd even owned these things in the first place? *Get over it, Kim*, I told myself. Be grateful for what you have, for what you still have, which is more than enough, more than you need, more than you imagined.

No one wants to see you cry over diamonds.

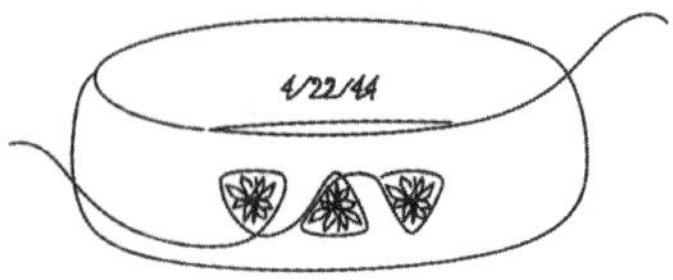

Grandma's Silver Wedding Band

Jewelry engraving dates back hundreds of years. Posy rings were popular during the fifteenth to seventeenth centuries. The name "posy" (also spelled "poesy" or "posie") comes from the French word "poésie" for poem. Initially, these rings had intricate designs and words engraved on the outside of the bands. But with time, the inscriptions became more personal and private, and were moved to the band's inside. Simple gold or silver rings carried phrases such as "God made us two one" or "Love me and leave me not." This represented a change in view from marriage as a contractual agreement between families to marriage as a bond of love and commitment between two people.

The practice of ring engraving still exists today, often with sentimental pieces, including heirlooms or wedding jewelry. It is common to include the initials of the couple or the wedding date.

chapter 10

2015, St. Louis, Missouri

"I think Grandma would have loved for you to have this," Aunt Jenn said as she reached across the kitchen table and handed me a small ring made of Florentine-brushed silver and three tiny, low-profile, triangular-shaped diamonds embedded into the metal.

My grandma had died earlier that year, a few months shy of her ninety-first birthday, after a long physical decline brought on by dementia. Sweet and joyful until the very end, she called everyone her angel. She left this world in the same way she'd lived in it.

Aunt Jenn pointed out the engraved inscription inside the band. April 22, 1944. To someone else, that date would be meaningless. For my grandma, it meant everything.

"I love it," I said, slipping the ring onto my right ring finger and finding a perfect fit. "What a special gift. A treasure. Thank you."

My left thumb skimmed along the silver, imagining the ring on my grandma's hand as she danced around the room, humming to her favorite Big Band music.

My grandparents were an integral part of my childhood. It would have been a completely different childhood without them because their presence intertwined all my memories. Even after we left St. Louis and settled in Colorado, they found a way to be a part of the big events of our lives—birthdays, holidays, graduations, and all the other celebrations. As a kid, I always looked forward to their visits. Whenever I knew they were coming, I sprinted down the stairs the moment the garage door opened, which signaled my dad's return from picking them up at the airport.

My grandma entered the house like a real-life Mrs. Claus. Before she even sat down or unzipped her jacket, she produced bags and boxes that contained small gifts or candy, all the things she had accumulated over the weeks or months we'd been separated, showing us how much she'd been thinking of us, and her gifts were always the most unique and thoughtful things, like spearmint Extra gum and Mike and Ike candies because she knew they were my favorites. Once she arrived, she buzzed around our house in the same way she buzzed around her own, taking care of the smallest things and looking out for others' needs and comforts.

My grandparents' visits enlivened the house. On school mornings, they always made it to the kitchen first. My grandpa sat at the table, drinking coffee and reading the newspaper, while my grandma stood behind the counter, deeply involved in the preparation of an elaborate breakfast.

"Good morning, sweetie," she'd say to me. "What can I get you? Do you want me to make you some toast? How about some bacon? Can I slice up some fruit for you? What would you like to drink? Frank—pick up some apple juice at the store, okay?" She'd slide a plate across the counter, already brimming with options she'd been preparing long before we woke up for the day.

"Kim, what is going on at school today?" my grandpa would ask, putting down the paper and peering at me over his readers. "What are you studying in history?" Or math. Or English. Or science. He never stopped learning or being curious. He'd ask to see my textbooks and papers, not missing a word.

I always looked forward to the end of the school day and coming home to see them. If I had homework or some other news—a minor hurt or a major accomplishment—they'd both immediately drop whatever they were doing and sit patiently, wanting to hear all the details of the day.

At bedtime, when my grandma came to say goodnight, she sat down on the edge of my bed as I lay under the covers. Her stories were my favorite, even the repeats, tales I'd heard numerous times, but I didn't care. I loved them all. And I especially loved hearing about her childhood, and her courtship and marriage with my grandpa.

Ruth Vasel's grandparents came to the United States from Germany and settled in St. Louis, Missouri. She attended school through eleventh grade but left for a job behind the counter at Kipp's Homemade Ice Cream and Candy Store before graduation.

One afternoon, a handsome sailor came into Kipp's and ordered an ice cream soda. Frank Intagliata became a regular customer, returning on many subsequent afternoons, more to see Ruth than for the ice cream. After a few weeks, she got in trouble with her boss for over-serving him, but she didn't mind because she had a serious crush on that lanky Sicilian guy. And that Sicilian guy had a thing for the green-eyed German girl behind the counter. Both were suckers for a uniform.

A year later, in 1944, while Frank was on leave during World War II, he married Ruth on a warm April morning. She wore her friend's ivory lace wedding dress and carried white lilies down the aisle. Frank wore US Coast Guard dress blues. They exchanged their vows at St. Columbkille's Church in south St. Louis near the Missouri River, and their reception took place at the Spanish Society, where they danced to Wurlitzer jukebox tunes. With each retelling of this story, my grandma's memories became my memories too.

After the war, Frank worked as a construction electrician and then as an electric apprentice instructor until he retired in 1987. Ruth volunteered at a local hospital as a candy striper—the perfect job for someone who loved talking to people. No one loved talking to people more than Ruth. They lived in a variety of apartments, including one with what my grandma described as "outside toilets" for ten dollars per month. They had three children: Michael, Jim, and Jennifer. In 1955, when Jenn was only eight months old, Frank and Ruth bought their first home in Affton, Missouri, for $13,500. Frank knocked $250 off the asking price because he offered to do the electrical wiring himself.

My grandpa met his best friends in elementary school, and their group stayed close for over eighty years. My grandma had a weekly visit to the same beauty parlor for decades. The Intagliatas never moved beyond the ten-mile radius within which they had spent their entire lives. They attended St. George's church for over fifty years.

My grandma took photos of everything and everyone all the time. And she meticulously documented the who, where, and when of every scene in her tight script on the back of every print. Her familiar cursive handwriting chronicled our family history.

When my grandma left Kipp's to get married, she didn't leave her legendary ice cream sodas behind, and she never lost her touch. More times than I can remember, and whenever we visited them at their home in St. Louis, my brothers and I saddled up to the canary-yellow counter in her kitchen and she'd bring out the supplies: vanilla ice cream, a two-liter plastic bottle of 7-up soda, chocolate syrup, cherries, tall fountain glasses, straws with accordion bends at the top that made right angles, and elongated spoons that could reach to the bottom of the glass. She stood across from us, at the ready and with love, just like she did with that handsome sailor a lifetime ago.

After my grandma died, my grandpa decided to move into assisted living. He put their house on the market, and my dad and his siblings began the long and arduous process of clearing out sixty years' worth of accumulation. In the clean-up, my aunt collected all the letters I had written to them throughout my life—from when I barely knew the alphabet until college when I sent them postcards covered with puffy stickers. They saved and laminated any piece of paper relevant to me: all the articles I wrote for my high school and college newspapers, every theater, sports, and scholastic awards program, and every graduation ceremony handout. In middle school, I wrote a poem about my grandma, which she framed and displayed on an end table in their family room. I wish I had kept it, not because it was a literary masterpiece (it definitely was *not)*, but because she loved it. A handful of words shoehorned into cringy rhymes, but she still loved it. My words mattered to her.

In the kitchen with my aunt, I slid the ring off my finger and held it to the light to better see the engraved inscription. On April 22, 1944, the ninth child of a Sicilian immigrant family married the fourth child of a German immigrant family. This ring symbolized the melding of two histories and cultures, and it was the first gift I had ever received that represented a generational line above my parents on the family tree. As the first grandchild and the only granddaughter, I knew I had a responsibility to my brothers and cousins—an obligation to keep the ring in the family and this legacy artifact safe.

Because someday, I'd be sitting at a table across from someone else, offering the ring with the words "I want to give this ring to you. It belonged to Ruth, my grandma. The date inside the band is her wedding date. She died in 2015. You would have loved her. She made the best ice cream sodas. And that's just the beginning of the story."

chapter 11

January 21, 2022

When everyone had left and unfamiliar voices no longer echoed in the house as they had for several hours, the boys slowly emerged from their rooms and joined us in the kitchen. They saddled up to the island, reaching for pieces of pizza. I grabbed a slice, too, and took a bite while standing over the cardboard box. It wasn't the night to fight over plates, crumbs, or even a side of vegetables.

With the house to ourselves, the boys felt free to ask questions. Even though they claimed they had no fears about what happened, their questions belied their bravery. This event marked their first interaction with crime or the police, discounting their dad's occasional speeding ticket and the time Cooper "accidentally" threw a rock into the neighbor's window.

"Are the police out looking for them now?"

"Do you think they had a gun?"

"Would they have killed us if we were home?"

"Will they come back?"

"Did they come into my room?"

"How long will they go to jail when they get caught?"

Ted and I took turns and explained what we knew, what we thought happened, and what we expected for the future. We knew people broke into our house and stole things from our closet. We thought it happened earlier that afternoon after

I'd left the house. The police had started an investigation and would give us updates. I did what I could to reassure the boys of their safety.

"They won't come back here. There's nothing left. They took what they were looking for, and they'd be stupid to come back to the same house. The police are looking now, and hopefully they'll catch them soon. But if they don't, the important thing is that we are all okay."

"Then why are you sad?" Cooper asked.

"Well, some of those things are really important to me—"

"Because they're worth money?"

"No, that's not why, but you're right that part makes it tough. But many of those things belonged to important people who are gone now, like Mimi and Grandma Ruth, so that's what makes them special."

"But those people aren't here anymore, so it's not like they'll be mad if you lost them," Cal added.

"That's true," I said, taking a beat to think about what he said. "I just miss them, and their things are all I have left, so they're like little reminders."

"But can't you just get new things? Dad's not gone. He can get you a new wedding ring, right, Dad?" Crosby looked at Ted.

"Good thinking, Cros." Ted smiled.

"That's another reason I'm sad about what happened, though. All of these things are special, too, because they remind me of important days in my life. Didn't you learn about symbols in school?"

"Yes, of course, Mom," Cooper said, "like in second grade."

"Okay, then. What's a symbol?" I pressed.

"Something that stands for something else," Cooper said, proudly.

"Like a skull and crossbones stands for death," Cal followed.

"Okay, yeah, well I was thinking more like a heart or rainbow, but you get the idea. Those pieces of jewelry are kind of like symbols for me."

"Crosby! I called that last slice!" Cooper shouted.

Because the burglary, and all evidence of it, was centralized in our bedroom and closet, I don't think the boys experienced the same apprehension or panic they would have felt had more of the house been trashed. Of course, the boys had immediately checked to make sure their belongings were in their proper places, which, in all three cases, meant entirely out of place. But they would have recognized someone else's ransack compared to their own. Thankfully, their rooms retained their original messes, with heaps on the floor and overflowing drawers of unfolded clothes and plastic toys, their candy stashes still hidden and unharmed. If their rooms had been upended or if our televisions or their electronic devices had been taken, the boys would have had a more personal and immediate reaction to the break-in. The concentrated loss meant a more concentrated reaction for me, but I saw a silver lining there, and I knew we had to look for silver linings.

I studied the boys as they sat and scarfed down their pizza, looking for signs of distress on their faces. But then Cal let out a huge belch, which in turn sent the other two into hysterics. Ted, surprised by the sound, spit out some of his drink.

"Cal!" I shrieked. "Come on. Manners."

"Sorry," he said while trying to keep a straight face. "Excuse me."

But the more he tried not to laugh, the louder he did, making the others lose their minds. Crosby nearly fell off the barstool and onto the floor.

I couldn't help but smile. It took a big ol' burp to break the tension, but that's exactly what we needed.

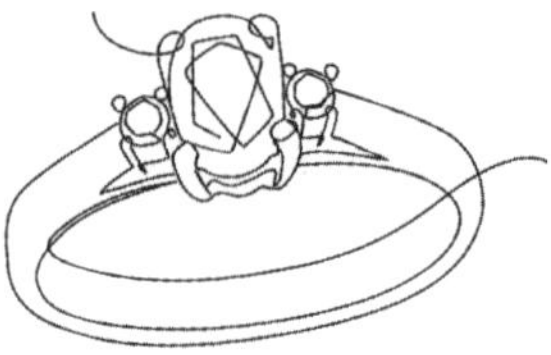

Silver Ring with a Blue Sapphire and Two Side Diamonds

Sapphires are resilient and long-lasting gemstones, the second hardest stone after diamonds. Sapphires are most well-known for their dark and vibrant blue shades, but the gem can be found in a spectrum of colors. The origin of the name "sapphire" is relatively unknown, but historians often link it to the Greek word "sappheiros," which means "blue."

Kings wore sapphires to keep them safe from evil or harm. One of the oldest stones in the British crown jewels is a sapphire located on the Imperial State Crown, and this stone is thought to have belonged to Edward the Confessor in the eleventh century AD. The most famous sapphire associated with British royalty, however, is likely Princess Diana's engagement ring, first given to her in 1981 by then Prince Charles. After Diana's death, her son William gave the ring to his betrothed Kate Middleton in 2010.

Sapphires have long histories of religious significance. They were included as one of the twelve stones on Aaron's breastplate in the book of Exodus, representing the twelve tribes of Israel, although some historians believe the actual stone was a lapis lazuli instead. During the Middle Ages, priests wore sapphires as a symbol of heaven, and lay people associated sapphires with blessings and abundance.

Today, sapphires are thought to bring peace and happiness.

chapter 12

2008, Denver, Colorado

"One year," I said, reaching my hand across the white tablecloth to grab one of Ted's sweet potato fries. "Can you believe it?"

He smiled. "I can."

The blue sapphire on my right hand caught the candlelight arc that spread across the table. A first wedding anniversary gift, the stone was set on a silver band with two petite round diamonds on either side of the sapphire.

I thought of the topaz ring my parents had given me for my eighteenth birthday. The bright, electric topaz blue contrasted with this deep, strong sapphire blue. I saw the sapphire as a kind of evolution on my finger.

"Things are going to look a lot different next year."

"It's a little terrifying, to be honest," Ted said, though with a grin.

"It's going to be great," I assured him. "I know it."

Two months earlier, I had stood upstairs in my bathroom, waiting for the result of a pregnancy test. With my hands on the edge of the counter, I leaned forward, eyes closed. After inhaling deeply, I looked down: two pink lines on a white stick.

Pregnant.

I always knew I wanted to be a mom, probably because my own mom set such a good example and we had such a close relationship. But my motherhood dream had existed more as a horizon plan—something to think about "sometime in the future."

That horizon started closing in soon after we got married. It was the next question in line.

You're dating? When's the engagement? You're engaged? When's the wedding? You're married? When's the baby?

Our wedding was only a few weeks before my thirtieth birthday, and I knew the tick on the maternal clock would only grow louder the longer we waited. Ted and I didn't have a plan for when we wanted to try and have kids, but we also didn't take any active steps one way or the other. If it happened, it happened. Turns out it happened.

On the night I took the test, Ted had gone out to a concert with friends. But my brother Adam had been staying with us for a couple of months while interviewing for jobs in Denver. As I stood at the sink upstairs, he watched television downstairs, blissfully unaware.

As soon as the positive line appeared, the information immediately felt like an overinflated balloon inside of me, ready to pop at any second. I ran to tell Adam.

"Really?" Adam said, searching my face, unsure how to react.

My eyes must have convinced him.

"Wow, congratulations!" he followed, in his own Adam kind of excitement, slightly above even.

I considered calling Ted but decided against it. This kind of reveal was too important for the telephone and not the conversation I wanted to have with Stone Temple Pilots raging in the background. I waited for him to get home, my head buzzing too loudly to fall asleep anyway.

When Ted walked in through the back door a little past midnight, I jumped up off the couch to greet him.

"I'm pregnant!" I announced.

He stood there, startled, and also seemingly unsure whether to celebrate. Later, he claimed the news didn't register at first because a night of drinking and heavy metal music dulled his receptors. He hadn't expected me to be awake, much less jumping up and surprising him. I wanted his excitement to match mine, but he needed a minute. His horizon plan didn't have the same deep roots as my plan did, and no ticking clock had ever interrupted his peace. But Ted came around soon enough.

Once we had an ultrasound to confirm, a grainy bean picture as proof, and a few more weeks to bobble the news back and forth in our hands until it didn't feel so hot, we told the rest of our families. When my mom saw the ultrasound picture, she looked up at me with wide eyes for confirmation. Then she screamed.

"Oh my gosh! A baby! Oh my gosh! A baby!"

Her excitement was the kindling I needed in those first few months, especially with the waves of nausea and morning sickness. She championed me and that baby every step of the way.

Some people are born to be grandmothers.

On that first anniversary dinner night, we celebrated the past year, but our sights were firmly set on the future. I didn't realize it then, but that sapphire stone would come to represent the boy who made me a mom. Later, the two sidecar diamonds would come to mean more abundance and blessing—a double portion, in fact.

This three-stoned ring told the story of the three best gifts of my life.

chapter 13

January 21, 2022

I suspected everyone.

A dryer repair person had been in our house earlier that morning, someone new. I found his name online and selected him over the other repairmen because he had same-day availability. He appeared nice enough when he came to the front door. We chatted as he followed me to the laundry room and, as far as I knew, he never left that room until he completed his work. He left following the same route he had entered: down the hall and out the front door. I never vacated the barstool at my kitchen counter while he was in the house until he finished the job and I paid him. My seat offered a direct view of my bedroom door. If he had gone in there, I certainly would have noticed.

But did I go to the bathroom? Or grab a snack from the pantry? If so, he could have dashed into my room for a quick scope. I don't think I did either of those things, but I couldn't say for sure, starting to doubt even my clearest memories.

Even if he didn't go into my room, he met Buddy and heard me say how he's the nicest dog. He'd gotten a lay of the house. And he knew I had plans to leave because he apologized for the work taking longer than he thought it would.

"It's fine," I said to him. "I don't need to leave here until 12:45."

I should never have offered that detail to a stranger.

The police immediately considered him the prime suspect because a brand-new person in the house and a burglary on the same day are beyond coincidental.

"What if you called him and said if he returned our things, I'd agree not to cooperate in any prosecution?" I had asked the officers earlier. "I only want to get my things back. If they simply mysteriously appear on my doorstep tomorrow, that could be the end of it."

If things had played out that way, it would have been a miracle. It would have been such a good story.

Rosary with White Beads

A rosary is a circular string of beads, each bead representing a particular prayer, used primarily in the Catholic tradition of Christianity. The beads are grouped in five sets of ten (called decades) with a larger or distinguishing bead separating each set. On the lower portion of the chain, a shorter strand extends from the circle, and a cross hangs at the very bottom of that strand. The rosary is used to help count and follow a sequence of specific prayers.

chapter 14

1985, Overland Park, Kansas

Dining room events signified importance, while everyday events took place at the kitchen table. One afternoon in May, when I was nine years old, I sat at the head of the dining table wearing a white dress with a lace overlay, like the white baptismal dress I wore eight years earlier and a preview of the white wedding dress I would wear twenty years later. An elbow-length veil made of white tulle framed my face. My family gathered around the table, including my grandparents, who had flown out from St. Louis to mark this historic day.

Everyone dressed up for the occasion. My mom wore a striking two-piece white ensemble with a black checkered design and shoulder pads—both categorically '80s. My mom's deep red and freshly permed hair coiled around her face. My grandma's short blonde hair also had tight curls, but hers came from late-night foam curler rolling sessions. The spirals under my veil came from my mom's handiwork with a small barrel curling iron. Three generations with curly hair, all in one place. My dad wore the same thing he wore every day to work—a dark suit—though this time, he'd ventured outside of his typical navy and black comfort zone with a colorful (well, burgundy, let's not get too crazy) tie. My mom managed to squeeze six-year-old Nick into khaki pants and secure a clip-on tie that left a six-inch gap above his belt buckle. Still a toddler, Adam donned one of my mom's hand-sewn gingham rompers with a little house embroidered on the chest and knee-high thin white socks and saddle shoes.

Grandma baked another special cake for the day, this one in the shape of a cross, with her characteristic white frosting and the words *God Bless You Kimberly* in pink icing. Sitting there, surrounded by my family, I basked in the attention on this very important day.

My grandma handed me a cardboard box with a pink bow. Inside, I found a white leather pouch cinched with a drawstring and *My First Rosary* imprinted in pink italics on the outside. The white and pink cake matched the decoration on the pouch, which I untied and turned upside down. A silver rosary with white beads fell into a pile in my palm. I grabbed one bead between my thumb and pointer finger and slowly untangled the long strand. My grandma smiled.

I knew the prayers and the sequence from Catholic school and catechism class but until this day, I had only practiced with borrowed rosaries. I loved the feel of the beads in between my fingers as I moved around the circle.

"Thank you, Grandma."

"You're welcome, sweetie. Now you have your very own."

We celebrated in the dining room because, earlier that day, I had lined up in the front of Holy Spirit Catholic Church with thirty other second graders to receive my First Communion. Families filled the pews, smiling and snapping photos.

My nerves tap-danced inside my stomach. We had been preparing for this event for months. Our teacher methodically took us through every moment—where to stand, what to say, what to do with our hands. The routine had been rehearsed countless times, and though I knew it all by heart, I still worried about slipping up and making a mistake.

When it came time for my turn, I looked up at the priest. He loomed large over me because he stood a few steps higher, and his layers of robes and vestments greatly increased his wingspan. The bright white square clerical collar interrupted the black of his shirt. The top ivory-colored vestment had brown stitching that ran down the front in the shape of a cross. I turned my palms up, laid my left over my right, and lifted both hands to my eye level, exactly how I had practiced, and waited for the priest to speak.

"This is the body of Christ," he said as he picked up one of the wafers from his shiny golden bowl and held it in front of my face.

"Amen," I replied. He set the wafer into my hands and then looked toward the person behind me, signaling me to move on.

I closed my palms to secure the quarter-sized disc and stepped to the right. The paper-thin wafer felt so fragile in my hands, like if I pressed it, it might crack into a thousand pieces. Moving to the side, I looked up and saw what the priest and all his layers had blocked—a towering wooden cross mounted on the wall behind the altar with a crucified Jesus sculpture suspended from it. I had noticed the cross before, of course, but only with passing glances. But that day, I tried memorizing the details. Jesus's ribs protruded out of his body. A draped shroud wrapped around his waist and a crown of thorns sat atop his head. His shoulder-length hair was parted down the middle. Two nails were strategically placed in the palms of his two hands, a third atop his left foot, pinning his feet together and to the wood, his gaze lowered to the ground.

In every Sunday Mass service before that day, I remained relegated to the pew while all the adults and "big kids" filed up for communion. I watched the lines proceed as I sat still and quiet because any moves or noises to the contrary received a glaring side-eye from my parents. We never sat close to the front because my squirrely brothers often required easy access to the exit where my dad or mom could pace the halls with them, so we sometimes opted instead for the cry room in the back of the church reserved for families with rowdy children. Jesus never appeared to be more than an outline up on that cross in the front, almost like he blended in with all the other furnishings.

But on that day, I stood close enough to see his face, his sculpted cheekbones and heavy-set eyes.

He looks so sad, I thought, as I placed the wafer on my tongue.

It disintegrated immediately into a chalky paste. I then stepped up to the deacon, who stood next to the priest, but on a lower step. The deacon's position, along with fewer vestment layers, made him loom as well, but not as large as the priest. The deacon held a gold chalice filled with grape juice masked as wine.

"This is the blood of Christ," he said.

"Amen," I replied.

He tilted the chalice toward me as I placed my lips on it and took a sip. I stepped to the side so the person behind me could have a turn. I looked back up at Jesus and made the sign of the cross.

In the name of the Father, the Son, and the Holy Spirit. Amen.

I paused there for a second, waiting for the important feeling. Even at nine years old, I knew this to be a significant life moment. I assumed something would stir inside of me because everyone told me it would. When I looked back up at Jesus, I expected him to look different than he had fifteen seconds earlier. But he looked the same. I also expected to feel differently inside than I had fifteen seconds earlier. But I felt the same. The aftertaste of the wafer and juice lingered on my tongue and the back of my throat. Dusty bits with a hint of grape.

I didn't meet God at the communion altar.

I didn't meet him in the confessional either.

My First Reconciliation took place the year after my First Communion. It had all the dread of being called to the principal's office. Unlike baptism and communion, I did not wear white and lace to this event or celebrate in the dining room afterward. I wore my red plaid school uniform skirt and a stiff white collared shirt and sat in the church pews alongside my classmates until a teacher called my name. Reconciliation gave me the opportunity to admit my wrongs, seek and receive forgiveness, and perform penance to demonstrate a changed heart. As a somber occasion, it didn't call for pink icing or gifts, because sin is somber. Yet this sacrament, like all other sacraments, marked a necessary rite of passage in my journey toward spiritual maturity, a better understanding of God, and a deeper faith.

Confessions took place in the back of the church, and three narrow arched doors were built for that purpose. The priest sat behind the middle door, and the confessor chose either the left or the right door. The left door opened to a space the size of a broom closet. A small window with a grated screen cut an opening on the room's right-hand wall, and a padded kneeler stood a few inches above the ground below the screen. This room, built for "private" confession, did not fully safeguard anonymity but gave the illusion it did.

Alternatively, the right door opened to another room, but this room did not have a dividing wall. Instead, the priest sat on his chair to the left of the room, with an empty chair to his right. Here, face-to-face confession took place.

The priest assumed his seat for the parade of confessors. If someone preferred private confession, he spoke through the screen, but if someone chose face-to-face, the priest swiveled in his chair to his other side so he could speak directly to the person.

For my first time, I chose the private option. The thought of admitting my wrongs head-on with a priest unnerved me, and the cloak of secrecy might not fully expose my guilt. Even at nine years old, I understood shame.

When the teacher called my name, my stomach dropped, and my heartbeat throbbed in my temples. I walked up and grabbed onto the brass doorknob. The door creaked as I opened it a few inches, enough to allow me to slip inside, and I shut the door behind me.

The cramped room made such a juxtaposition with the vaulted ceilings of the giant church outside it. It oddly reminded me of *Alice in Wonderland*, though the room did the shrinking, not the girl. I felt intimidated, which didn't fit the room, considering its pocket size, because of an inability to pinpoint what kind of feelings were the right ones. The only light shining into the dark space came from a stained-glass cut-out design on the top of the door, the colored tiles gathered the light from the expansive windows of the church on the other side and cast a prism of reds and blues. I knelt and the priest slid the square metal door open to reveal the grated screen. Our heads were only inches away from each other, separated by the mesh wire. Like with my First Communion, I rehearsed my lines many times to be sure not to screw them up.

"Bless me, Father, for I have sinned. This is my first confession."

"Proceed," the priest responded.

Per my teacher's instruction, I confessed three sins. "I lied to my parents. I fought with my brothers. I spoke in a disrespectful way. For these and all my sins, I am truly sorry." Not sweet, but short.

Those particular sins were safe and ordinary, and I thought if the priest heard the same kind of sins from other kids, I'd blend in with them. This was no time to stand out. Thankfully, the priest didn't probe for any specifics. He had a long line of confessions still to go.

He assigned me penance, a set of prayers, and he drew a cross in the air with the edge of his hand, symbolizing the absolution of my sins. I made the sign of the cross in tandem with him, stood up, and slipped out of the room as quickly as I could, shutting the door behind me. The whole experience lasted no more than three minutes, though it felt like hours. I imagined that speaking to the priest would be the same as speaking directly to God himself, but that didn't ring true. The whole experience felt more heavy than holy. But I didn't know any better, in the way I didn't know any better with all the other sacraments, or religion in general. I simply followed the path laid out before me.

I returned to my place in one of the pews and waited while the rest of my classmates took their turns. Guiding the kneeler gently to the ground, I tried not to make the loud thump that occasionally reverberated as things do in an open, mostly vacant church. I slid forward, my knees pressed into the faux leather-covered foam pad, closed my eyes to a squint, and rattled off the prayers in my head.

That first confession and all subsequent confessions followed the same pattern, saying and doing the required things. I completed the penance but never really trusted in the forgiveness. I stuck to confessing the run-of-the-mill sins and burying the more specific, shameful ones, thinking that if I hid them from the priest, I hid them from God, and therefore avoided getting into trouble with anyone, especially God.

Like the time I dropped my cousin's wrapped birthday gift and heard something shatter inside. No one saw me, so I quietly slipped out of the room and later blamed it on my brother Nick. Or in elementary school, when I sat in silence as a kid was bullied by other kids. I didn't contribute, encourage, or join them, but I certainly didn't oppose them either. I merely merged with the group, not wanting to ruffle any feathers and risk exclusion.

I couldn't confess the real sins. What if God wouldn't love me if he really knew me? Thankfully the priest never took notes or probed for more details, so I figured my plan worked. The priest would never be the wiser, and therefore neither would God.

Faith had always been a part of my life—imposed in my childhood, held at arm's distance as a young adult, temporarily abandoned in my mid-20s, and a guiding and eclipsing force since age 30. I used to think God showed up differently as I grew older, but I learned I simply showed up differently to him. God wouldn't be God if he changed.

My parents grew up in the Catholic church because their parents and grandparents grew up in the Catholic church. They attended Catholic grade school, wore uniforms, and learned from nuns. Their families, like many Catholic families, never missed Mass on Sundays. My grandpa attended almost every day of his adult life. My parents replicated their Catholic upbringings for us. We wore the uniforms and learned from nuns.

We also had a Brother.

Brother Timothy taught middle school math and German. He smoked and rarely smiled, but in my experience, most Catholic school teachers smoked and rarely smiled, so those things did not stand out as unique. Brother Tim commanded the classroom as he paced up and down the rows. I don't remember him smashing a wooden pointer stick on desks as he passed by them, but if anyone would do such a thing, it would have been Brother Tim. I knew nothing of his life outside of school or what drew him to the brotherhood or the classroom, and merely assumed he lived a Grinch-style existence. I feared him with the same fear I had for other authority figures like coaches, teachers, and parents. But anyone associated with the church clicked my people-pleasing instincts into overdrive because of the moral high ground that came with the job.

I tried impressing Brother Tim in the same way I tried impressing the priests in the confessional by pretending to be the person they wanted me to be, or at least the person I thought they wanted me to be, sacrificing authenticity for subterfuge.

My Catholic upbringing provided structure in my life and tangible introductions to God, knowledge, ritual, and consistency. But in the end, for me, it fell short when it came to relationship. I desperately wanted to experience a God who saw and knew and loved me. A God who accepted me for me, and a God who welcomed honesty. Every Sunday, I stepped up for communion and stared at Jesus on the cross, expecting him to feel closer. Every time I confessed my sins and completed my penance, I expected to feel forgiven and less shameful. Every time I tried gaining Brother Tim's admiration or the admiration of the priests or any one of the religious authorities, I expected to feel more worthy and accepted. Every time I moved across the beads on my white rosary, I expected to feel closer to God. But the rituals, the people, and the structures always seemed to get in my way. The beads threw me off track.

Though my experience of God did not extend beyond my religion, I don't blame the religion. It was always only supposed to be an introduction and a gateway, never a substitute. I yearned to connect with God, to feel his presence in an intimate and personal way.

It happened when I was twelve years old.

The gray and clouded sky created silver swaths of shadows over the grass, rearranging themselves as the clouds shifted. A storm approached, but it didn't deter my walk toward the playground, which was thankfully empty at the time.

I stepped over the low wooden edge that bordered the perimeter, and immediately, my tennis shoes drilled into the pebble gravel. The swings gently stirred in the slight breeze, chains melodically clinking against each other. I climbed to a platform by the green slide and paused, standing still, searching for a sign of God in the sky, because that day, for the first time in my life, I wanted to ask him something. Only him. Not him via the teachers or the priests or the borrowed prayers. I listened for God but heard nothing, only the swish of the wind. I searched for some sign of him but saw nothing, only the gathering clouds. With eyes clenched shut and all the earnestness I could muster, I said in a low but discernable voice: "God, please let me fly."

I repeated the request, slowly, articulating each word, out loud, in case he didn't hear my thoughts.

"Please. Please. Please."

Moving to the edge of the platform and curling my toes around it, I looked one more time up at the clouds and then toward the ground before crouching into a tight ball, closing my eyes, and repeating the same words.

"God, please let me fly."

Somewhere deep inside of me, I truly believed in this precise moment that God, and only God, could make something like this possible. For what might have been the first time in my life, I believed in the power of God. I pushed on the balls of my feet and launched myself from the platform, expecting to swoop up like a kite in the wind.

I did not swoop up like a kite in the wind.

A half-second later, I felt the edges of the gravel poke up into the bottom of my sneakers when I landed, with a thump, on the ground. I opened my eyes and immediately looked back up into the sky for another sign. My brow furrowed as I stood up and kicked off some of the pebbles that had landed atop my shoes on impact.

"Let's go again," I said, including God in this pursuit.

Climbing back up, I wondered if a lack of conviction on the first try had prevented success. Closing my eyes and pressing my palms together, I prayed my first honest prayer.

"God, only you have the power to make me fly. Because you are God, and I believe in you. So please let me fly. Amen."

Another jump. And another immediate landing on the ground.

Brushing the dust off my pants, I considered whether God wasn't going to let me fly because I chose a platform height only five feet off the ground, low enough that I could fall without injuring myself. Maybe I needed to up the stakes and, therefore, demonstrate a greater belief.

I considered this for a moment, standing somewhere in between risk and abandonment, and then climbed up to the highest platform and looked down. The fall was about twelve feet, but it looked like double that from the top. If this didn't work, I could get really hurt.

"God, I believe you can do this. But I also believe you might be telling me this is a dumb idea."

I climbed back down and started walking home.

I didn't fly that day, or any other day, but something changed inside of me on that platform. Something changed because I called to the God I knew in my heart, rather than the God in the external structures and rituals. I wanted something from a place so deep inside of me, and somehow, I knew the only one who could meet me there had to be him. For the first time in my life, I experienced him in a true, close, personal way. I called, and I expected and believed he would answer me.

Deep calls to deep at the roar of your waterfalls.

This verse from the Psalms explains what happened at the park that day. I yearned for something, and I called on God. For the first time, my deep called to his. Only he had the power to make something so preposterous happen, and something inside of me knew this information as if it had been there from the beginning. It didn't take a sacrament or a rosary or a priest for me to realize it; it had been there all along.

Before that day, when I thought of Jesus, I thought of the sculpture hanging on a cross behind an altar—impenetrable and impersonal. It would take many more years for me to understand what it all meant—what Jesus did on that cross and why. But at the playground on that cloudy day when I was twelve years old, I tapped into a God grander than my religion, a God outside of human constructions, a God who had always been there, close, patiently waiting for me to call to him.

Twenty-five years after that afternoon at the playground, while searching for something in my attic, I came across a small cedar box. The box held all sorts of artifacts of my faith, including my baptismal candle, a *Precious Moments* prayer book, my Confirmation stole, and the miniature leather pouch with *My First Rosary.*

I turned the pouch over, and the white beaded chain spilled into the palm of my hand, the same way it did that special day in the dining room. The silver chain had rusted into a black hue, and the beads had a yellow tinge. I ran my fingers along them and tested my memory of the prayers. The rhythm of the words and the feel of the beads brought me back to those early days of faith, days when I tried to make sense of God. But this time, as I whispered the words, I said them slowly, without jumping from bead to bead at the rapid pace I'd perfected over all those years. Instead, my fingers paused on the spaces in between the beads, in the links of the chain.

Deep calls to deep in the roar of your waterfalls.

Without the chain, a rosary is simply a pile of beads. Without the relationship, religion is simply a pile of words. I never needed the things to find God because God was never in the things.

chapter 15

January 21, 2022

Once the boys had finished their dinner, they headed back to their rooms. I turned on the sink and started rinsing the dishes.

Ted came up and stood next to me. "I got this," he said, grabbing the glass out of my hand.

"Thanks," I said, drying my hands with a dishtowel. "I think I'll go back to the closet." There was something I wanted to check.

I found the cedar box in the corner on the floor, open and lying on its side, its contents a jumbled mess.

Crouching down, I lifted the faded leather pouch from under the pile and turned it over. Empty.

They took the rosary, I thought. It had been decades since I'd even looked at it. Why did they take it? It wasn't worth anything. It made no sense.

But then again, nothing about that day made sense. The burglary rattled my faith in humanity and my confidence in the decency and goodness of others. A sense of bitterness had already taken root, and it had only been a few hours.

I closed my eyes and prayed.

It went something like this.

God, this is one of those deep calls to deep moments. All these feelings are coming up, and I don't know what to do about them. It's confusing and overwhelming. I'm trying to focus on what's important here, that everyone's safe, but I still feel unsettled and need to find some peace. Because I'm really, really angry right now, fearful, and just so very sad.

I know this is a broken world we live in, full of hard, sharp pieces that sometimes cut us. Today reminded me of that.

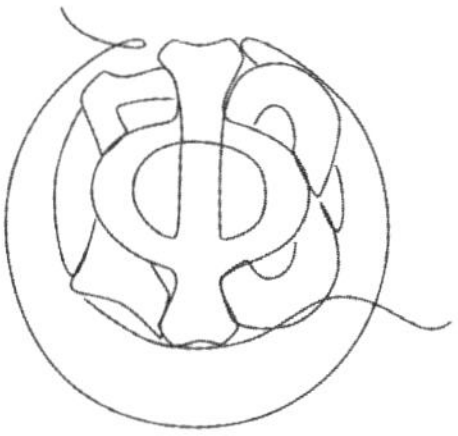

Gamma Phi Beta Sorority Pin

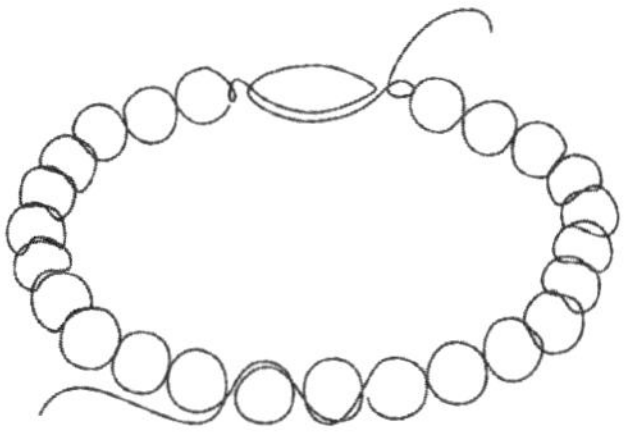

Pearl Bracelet with an Antique Silver Clasp

A collegiate sorority pin, also called a badge, carries the official insignia of the sorority. A new member receives the pin after completing a pledge period and an initiation ceremony. This custom has been a ritual in Greek organizations since they began in the nineteenth century. Among many other symbolic objects, the pin represents connection and belonging within a particular group.

Although classified as gemstones, pearls are unique because they come from living creatures. Mollusks make pearls to protect themselves against irritants or debris that penetrate their shells. They do this by exuding layer upon layer of shell material called nacre. After years, this material builds up and becomes a pearl. Pearls are a metaphor for the idea that something beautiful can emerge from hardship.

chapter 16

1996, San Diego, California

The women all stood together in a large and dark room, lit only by candlelight. I stepped forward from the circle when my name was called. Words were exchanged, an oath sworn, and a pin secured. I slid backward into my spot in the circle as the next person took her turn. The pin made it officially official. I belonged. Not only for a year, or some other determined fraction of time, I belonged to Gamma Phi Beta for life.

As I stood there and waited for the rest of my fellow pledges to be initiated, I glanced down and pulled at the bodice of my white dress to have another look at the pin. Tracing the Greek letters, ΓΦΒ, I pressed the pin down, back onto my heart.

I'd always wanted a sister. Now, I had dozens. That promise of belonging is what had drawn me to the sorority. The invitation to stay is what kept me there.

For that, I blame *The Babysitters Club.*

The Babysitters Club books, written by Ann M. Martin, dominated my life from the age of 11 to 14. The Club originally had four members—Kristy, Mary Anne, Claudia, and Stacey—but over the years, they added and lost a few others. Miraculously, all the girls only aged one year over the course of the series. *Sweet Valley High* books also played heavily in my rotation during those preteen years, but Elizabeth and Jessica Wakefield were too pretty, too popular, and thus unrelatable.

The Babysitters, though, seemed more within my reach. I didn't admire or share their entrepreneurial spirits; I simply loved the idea of a tight-knit group of friends.

Though babysitting is the named enterprise in the series, friendship is the overarching theme. Each character faces different challenges, including health issues, parents' divorce, moving, and unrequited love. Yet they continually come back to each other, closing the circle with unconditional acceptance and loyalty.

I had always been a floater in school, never truly belonging to such a singular group. There were times in middle and high school that people welcomed me into their folds, but it was never a secure feeling, and it didn't happen every day. I never really knew whether I belonged inside or out, so I stayed on the edges, always moving back and forth between different groups.

It meant I had a lot of different friends, people who were interested, like me, in a variety of activities and sports, as well as getting good grades. That allowed me to put a positive spin on my insecurity, and, later in life claim to prefer the freedom and independence the outskirts offered. But honestly, more often I felt alone. Thank goodness social media did not exist during my formative years, because photographic evidence of exclusion would surely have catapulted my anxieties. Fear of missing out, FOMO, had always existed, but without the ability to document it, society hadn't yet found the right name.

Lunchtime in the high school cafeteria served as the ultimate test of my social position. Sometimes, I sat down alone at a table, and others joined me. Other times, I walked into the cafeteria and heard the precious words, "Kim—here!" as someone motioned for me to join them and slid over on the bench to make room. A few inches can make a drastic difference in a person's afternoon.

But that seat never felt like a guarantee for me and greatly depended on the season, the sports team, the science class lab partner, or whatever external force governed at the time. It got to the point where if I didn't see any blatant vacancies or hear an invitation, I'd simply turn on my heels, head to the library, and eat lunch on my own in a cubicle. This became a skill I mastered during high school, but it also served me well at obligatory dinners and gatherings later in life. I've spent many a cocktail hour hiding in a bathroom stall.

Social anxiety did, however, come with some benefits. I learned how to shape-shift, turning into whoever I needed to be to fit in with the group, whether it be teammates, neighbors, or study partners. Sometimes, I played the goofball, and other times, the serious student. Sometimes, I played the athlete, and other times, the wannabe. I became a chameleon so as not to feel alone, aligning my identity to gain entrance.

The promise of belonging is what drew me to the sorority. The offer of a "sisterhood" provided solid ground and an open, long-standing invitation. This group made room for me, and the entire rush process proved they wanted me to be there. We formed a circle and made a promise that forever locked me inside. I had a pin to prove it.

But after college graduation, the pin lost its luster, and I rarely had reason to remove it from its maroon velvet sack. Occasionally, I would pull it out and trace the Greek letters with the pad of my finger, exactly as I'd done that night at the initiation ceremony.

That pin promised something. And for a short time, the sorority delivered what I'd needed. My friends inside that circle certainly helped that girl who had stood inside the Del, feeling stuck, lonely, and desperately missing her mom. The sorority filled a gap and gifted me a connection during those first difficult years away from home.

But in the end, that gift didn't last. Because it wasn't built on something real.

2018, Denver, Colorado

In the spring of 2018, my dear friend Alea gifted me a bracelet, a beautiful chain of cream-colored pearls strung together and connected with a silver clasp. Alea and I met in a women's Bible study and served on the leadership team together. Her love language is gift-giving, and not just any gift, always the most thoughtful and meaningful gifts. She once made me a pair of yellow mittens and said she prayed for me while knitting them. Who does that? Only Alea. She gave me that pearl bracelet to celebrate my first year with the class.

In 2017, Alea was seriously injured in a snowmobile accident. During her months-long hospital stay and intensive rehabilitation, our leaders' team closely followed her story, prayed for her, and did what we could to support her during what became a true uphill battle.

Her gift of the pearl bracelet carried significance on so many levels.

The groups that offer true belonging are the ones that offer it in the hard times. Life has a stripping mechanism when things get messy. Like peeling an onion. Identities are laid bare. There was a time in Alea's life when she needed strength and protection, and there were times after that when I did too. The same circle of women who prayed for Alea, who prayed for her on their knees on dirty old carpet in the back room of a church, were the same people who, four years later, gathered close and prayed over me when people broke into my home and stole my precious things.

Every time I clasped that bracelet on my wrist, I thought not only of Alea but of friends like her. The kind of people who show up when irritants or debris sneak into our shells. The kind of friends who bring food when you bring home a new baby and when you lose someone you love. The kind of friends who don't have easy answers to things like 9/11 or school shootings or pandemics but are willing to sit in the sadness. The kind of friends who show up for the good times but also stay for the hard times. Everyone should be so fortunate to have a pearl or two. And if there are enough for a whole strand, well, that's a good life. That's a circle that lasts.

chapter 17

January 21, 2022

My knees creaked as I stood up and walked out of the closet into the bedroom. Black powder remained on the door frame where the police had dusted for fingerprints. It looked like chimney soot on the white trim.

They must have walked right here, right where I'm standing, I thought as I imagined them here, face-to-face with me.

I wonder if they touched this bed. My hand reflexively shivered as I placed it on the quilt. I sat down at the end of the bed and focused on the moonless night. *This is where they broke in*, I thought.

Suddenly, their faces appeared out of the shadows on the other side of the glass. Looking in, they pounded the glass door with their fists. Their eyes met mine. Every sensation in my body sparked, and I leaped up to stand.

They disappeared.

I moved right up to the glass. Nothing but black. *It's only your imagination. You're seeing things.* I shook my head and took a deep breath. *Relax. No one is there.*

Still, I could not shake the feeling of violation, that vivid picture of their faces and the pulsating sound of their hands hitting the glass.

I hurried to the family room, needing to get out of the bedroom. Sports announcers and intermittent whistles blared from the television. Ted sat on the couch, propped up by pillows, staring at his phone. Scanning the corners of the room, I made sure the kids were not within earshot.

"I don't know if I can sleep here tonight," I told him. "I keep imagining them watching me on the street, or at the door or in our room, or their hands all over my things."

He looked up. "Do you want to go to a hotel?"

With a sigh, I sat down beside him on the couch, bent forward with my elbows on my knees as I propped my head in my hands.

Yes, I thought. I did. But the notion of packing bags, figuring out Buddy, and rounding up the kids overwhelmed me. I didn't have the energy.

"No. It's too late. Plus, we've assured the boys there's no need to worry. If we leave, it will give them a reason to be scared."

"Do you want to go by yourself? I can stay here with them. We can make up a reason you need to go."

"No. I think we should be together. I don't think there is a real threat. It's just an unshakable feeling. My imagination is all over the place. How can I get them out of my head?"

Ted turned off the television.

"They're not coming back," he said. "They already took what they wanted. There's no reason they'd come again and risk getting caught." He put his arm around me and drew me toward him.

"You're right," I said, nodding into his shoulder. "I know that's right."

Of all the emotions of the day, fear proved to be my greatest struggle. I hated worrying about my family's safety. When was the last time I felt so scared? I couldn't remember.

"I'll get through it." I gave him a quick squeeze before I stood. "I may not sleep at all tonight, but I'll get through it."

They took my things. I'd be damned if they took my sense of safety in my own home.

"I'll get through it," I repeated under my breath while walking back into the bedroom. I stepped over the pieces of the sliding door but felt no impulse to clean or sweep them up.

I scooted my nightstand back into its place next to the bed and thought of stashing something in the drawer to protect us if they came back. Nothing it held at that moment would suffice for a suitable weapon. I rifled through books, eye masks, cords, old journals, and fifteen different lip balms.

Glancing around the room, I wondered about a potential weapon. We didn't own any guns. Our kids didn't play baseball. A lacrosse stick would be impossible to hide. Being able to hide it seemed important, maybe because I felt I should hide my fear. I considered putting a knife in the drawer, but the thought of using one made me want to vomit, so instead, I brainstormed household items that could be used as protection. Maybe a vase? Or a heavy picture frame? Where did I put that mace spray my mom gave me years ago?

A hammer flashed in my mind. We had one of those—the tool kit! Yes, tools would be perfect. I walked out of the room and into the garage and dragged the big yellow box from one of the shelves. The broken latch flopped as it clanked on the stiff plastic. I rooted through the contents and pulled out both the hammer and a wrench. I sat back on my heels and noticed my hands shaking. What was I thinking?

A wrench? Really?

My mind went to one of my favorite childhood board games: Clue.

Colonel Mustard. With the wrench. In the Billiards Room.

I laughed, despite myself, and the laughter lifted my heavy spirit.

In the span of only a few hours, I had managed to go from a person who rarely locked her front door to one who contemplated the weapon she could stash next to her bed in case of a home invasion.

I double-checked the locks on all the doors and windows and turned on all the patio outside lights. The LED lights shone on the house's white stone exterior, and the house glowed like a supermoon.

We need to install motion sensor lights on the sides of the house. Add it to the list. Metal bars for all the sliding door tracks. More window coverings. I should change the locks and garage keycode now. Do we have a Neighborhood Crime Watch? I should start one. Tomorrow, I'll call the alarm company and request cameras with the security system. Add it to the list.

The police told us jewelry thieves typically target bedrooms and closets because they know those places are where people get dressed. I decided to move things out of there, so I went back into the closet and stared at all the piles. I bent down and grabbed the stack of our passports I had set aside. They needed a new hiding place.

Not in the closet. Too easy.

I walked out of my bedroom and toward the kitchen, opened a cabinet, and considered sliding them by the cookbooks. Or I could tuck them in the office, between books on the shelf. But the office might also be a target.

Everything seemed to be in the wrong place. My laptop couldn't stay in the office. Too obvious. Or my purse on the kitchen counter. Too convenient. We couldn't leave cash in our closet or our documents in file cabinets. We needed a heavy-duty safe. Or would an inconspicuous shoebox be a better option?

I felt the urge to relocate everything, to create my own upending.

Silver Necklace with an Aquamarine Pendant

The name aquamarine is derived from the Latin words "water of the sea," reflected in the stone's blend of blue and green colors. Aquamarine was believed to come from the treasure of mermaids and was used to bring good luck and protection to fishermen and sailors. Because of its pure and tranquil color, the stone has also been linked to youth and happiness. Aquamarine is found in locations throughout the world, including the Colorado mountains.

The origin of birthstones dates back many centuries. Some scholars link birthstones to the twelve stones of Aaron's breastplate in the Book of Exodus in the Bible, representing the twelve tribes of Israel. Others claim specific stones relate to astrological birth charts or zodiac signs. The modern tradition of birthstones became formalized in 1912 when the National Jeweler's Association standardized the list of stones and corresponding months of the year. Aquamarine, for example, is the birthstone for March.

chapter 18

2009, Denver, Colorado

A "push present" is a gift a partner or spouse gives a new mother after the birth of a child. Anyone who has had to perform this particular type of pushing would agree it is more than worthy of a gift.

In my case, the "pushed" child was our son, Calvin, who entered this world on March 5, 2009. To commemorate this extraordinary event and the extraordinary effort on the part of the pusher (me), Ted gave me a beautiful necklace with an aquamarine pendant. The pale aqua color of the stone matched Cal's bright eyes and his March birthdate.

Though I did not plan for (and did not want) a "natural" birth, I did not have time for an epidural, despite screaming for one throughout the delivery process. All the information we learned in those prep classes about breathing and the different stages of labor and positions evaporated into the sterile hospital air as soon as the first real contraction came.

"Put him back in!" I shrieked. "I want my epidural!"

"Well, we see the head, so it's too late for that. He's coming," said the doctor, her words muffled by a hospital mask.

Despite the chaos of the ordeal, one mid-birth moment remained crystal clear. As the baby started crowning, Ted asked the doctor whether he should move his car because he parked in an emergency spot and worried about his laptop in the back seat. I stopped mid-push to glare at him.

"Are you kidding me?" I cried through clenched teeth.

"What?" he said quizzically and completely unaware. "Bad time to ask?"

Ted also claimed he wore "the first shirt I could grab" as we rushed out of the house to the hospital. His T-shirt collection occupied two full shelves in the closet, all meticulously folded and stacked in a way that defied reason. Nobody folded a shirt like Ted did. Though he never worked retail, he would have been a manager's dream, tidying up piles of folded shirts after customers rummaged through to find a particular size. He could have picked any shirt out of the dozens he owned, but he chose a maroon shirt with a picture of a rooster on it with one large word underneath in all caps: COCKY.

Every photo we have of Cal's birth, including that iconic post-birth hospital bed photo with mom holding the newborn baby in a tiny striped beanie hat and swaddled in a blanket, as dad leans over and smiles, Ted is wearing a shirt that says COCKY.

A nurse poked her head inside and asked if it was okay to let our parents come in because "we have a very anxious and excited crowd out there waiting to meet their grandson." On Ted's side, Cal is the fourth oldest grandchild, preceded by our two nephews and one niece. But Cal is the first grandson on my side, so we had a couple of grandparents born that day too.

My mom stayed for a short time after we'd settled in our room. She held Cal in a chair next to my hospital bed and sang sweet lullabies to him. She said she'd never forget his eyes that night, falling into a new kind of love with this baby, a love without the responsibility or expectation a parent's love requires, a love without the fine print. A brand-new grandma with a brand-new grandbaby.

Details of that experience fell into a haze in the days and weeks after Cal's birth. Still, the memory of my mom rocking my newborn son became one of the touchstone moments of my life, something I'd come back to many times over the years, especially after she was gone.

Two days later, we brought Cal home from the hospital. Placing him in his dark mahogany crib with red and blue plaid bumpers, I thought of all the hours I had sat in the oversized denim-upholstered rocker leading up to those days, staring at the crib and dreaming of this baby boy I'd yet to meet.

The months that followed blur together in my memory, but I do remember one sleepless night as I rocked with him in that chair, trying to soothe him back to sleep. A clock ticking loudly on the wall made the only sound in the house. Ted and what felt like the rest of the world slept while Cal stared up at me. I held him in the crook of one arm and, with my other hand, reached up and felt the aquamarine pendant as it dangled from my neck. The stone reminded me of the day he was born and the fury of his debut into this world. I dropped my hand and brushed my thumb across his forehead as I stared at him and considered this little clean slate, a flawless open-ended possibility, as his chest moved up and down with every breath.

I workshopped a silly poem in that dark room, humming the lines as I searched for the right words. He provided such a captive audience; those aquamarine eyes watched me with the kind of intensity only a brand-new human being could have. Everything dazzles and mystifies at the very first sight. I kept working on his poem aloud over the following days and weeks, in the many (and there were many) hours we spent together in that room. Just the two of us.

Who will you be?
My sweet boy, my little one.
I think about days and years ahead
On this journey we've begun.
You lie so small here in my arms
With a slightly furrowed brow.
I wonder many things about you
As we rock together now.
I wonder who you'll look like
Whose reflection will we see?
Your dad's nose or grandma's eyes
What will you take from me?

When will you mark your milestones
To smile, crawl, and walk?
What will be the words you'll choose
When you finally learn to talk?
Oh sweet boy, my little one,
I hold you here so tight.
I'd like to stop time now
To keep you in my sight.
But you will grow, and you will learn
You will come into your own.
You will find your joys and strengths
Your trek is yours alone.

Your whole life lies ahead of you
But here you only sleep and dream.
I hold tight this single moment when
Things are as simple as they seem.
But my mind drifts beyond this room
And down your path with you.

As you discover your own self
And learn what's truly true.

I wonder what interests you'll discover
And who your friends will be.
What will bring you the most joy?
Who will set your spirit free?
How will you decide
The choices that you'll make?
What will you overcome
And what risks will you take?

Who will share your first kiss
And who will break your heart?
Where will you have to pivot?
When will you need a new start?
I look at you with hope and awe
Your potential undefined.
How can I help you find your way
And help your light to shine?

For I am already proud of you,
And I'm proud of who you'll be.
I hope one day in the many ahead
You'll also be proud of me.
I wish you every joy in this world
I wish all your dreams come true.
You've opened up my eyes and heart
My little boy, how I love you.

Ten years later, I rediscovered the poem and the memory in a creased piece of notebook paper stuck inside a manila file folder wedged between old tax returns. As soon as I unfolded the paper and began reading, the words transported me back to that room, rocking in the big blue chair and gently humming the words of my dreams over my son.

Someday, I thought, *I'd give this poem back to him*. Someday, when he became the man that I had dreamed he'd be. I re-typed it and saved it in a computer file backed up to the cloud, to be sure I never lost it again. Those words connected me to a person, a place, a time, and a hope-filled vision for the future.

Words can be reliable safekeepers. Better, perhaps, than a necklace.

chapter 19

January 21, 2022

Late in the evening, the stack of passports weighed heavily in my hand. I didn't know where to put them or where to put anything. It's too late to rearrange all this stuff right now, I thought. I walked back into the closet and placed the stack on a shelf. *I'll figure it out tomorrow; there are so many things to figure out tomorrow*. My list started jumbling in my head.

The room fell quiet until I heard the familiar *clack, clack, clack* of Buddy's nails on the wood floor. He stopped at the closet door and stared at me. I swear he had remorse on his face.

"Hey, Buds," I said.

At the sound of his name, he took a few more steps toward me. I parted some of the obstacles on the floor to create a path for him. He gingerly moved forward, but when he came within inches of me, he stopped. He stood still, almost as if he sensed the solemnity of the scene. The only movement in the room was the sweep of his long tail in the air as it swished reflexively back and forth. I squatted down to bring my face close to his and rested my forehead onto his as he pressed his forehead into mine and squinted his eyes. I draped my arms around his neck.

"I'm so glad they didn't hurt you, Buddy," I whispered into his floppy ear.

Not that I ever seriously considered the possibility of a break-in, but I thought for sure the presence of a 200 pound

Great Dane would make any wannabe thief reconsider. Anyone who looked in the window and saw him would surely immediately turn and walk away. Surely, they would.

Buddy startled every delivery person and unsuspecting neighbor who rang our front doorbell, and their reactions upon seeing him were predictable. Jaw drop, two steps back, and a "Woah, that's a big dog." He rarely barked, but when he did, the sound boomed throughout our entire house. Every single time (and I mean every single time) we went for a walk, someone stopped and made some version of the following comments: "He's a pony!" or "You need a saddle for that guy!" or "Which way is the stable?" People regularly crossed the street to the other side or choked up on the leashes of their own dogs in protective stances, ready for Buddy the Beast to pounce.

But upon meeting him, it took only a few seconds to realize that he was as gentle as he was giant. He nuzzled up to anyone, stranger or not, with his signature Great Dane lean, longing for a pet. The furthest thing from a guard dog and more feline than canine, Buddy preferred napping to all other things, except eating his food (or anyone's food wherever he could reach: the table, counter, and occasionally out of the trash).

Maybe the people who broke into our house had been inside it before that day (if they were connected to the construction or the dryer repair) and would have quickly observed Buddy's docile nature and his laid-back attitude toward people coming and going. They would have realized it even if they hadn't met him if they had spent any time watching our house and observed his mild manners while he stood in the front yard. Or, even if they didn't see Buddy until they stepped foot inside our home, they still might have quickly surmised his sweet-tempered nature.

I knew for certain that if someone came in and tried to hurt anyone in our family, Buddy would protect us. But without an immediate threat, Buddy would never do more than ask someone to pet him.

I wanted to believe these people had not been inside our house before the day of the burglary because then it would have been less of a violation of trust, as if there were an unspoken, implicit social contract that when a person enters a house, they won't return and steal things.

It was possible that Buddy'd squeezed himself into whatever space he could find and leaned into them as they were dumping my jewelry into bags. I could also imagine him slumping down and sleeping through the entire event, right there on the floor next to them as they looted through my things. Another bet is that by the time they got down to business without paying him any attention, he simply sashayed back to his bed in the family room, curled up into the tightest ball a mini horse can muster, and drifted back to sleep, slightly miffed at being underappreciated but also entirely unconcerned.

Ever since that first phone call with Ted, I pictured these thieves with so many different faces, different statures, and different clothes. I imagined the different locations where they watched as they waited for me to leave, and the different things they said to each other with every discovery. I imagined their hands all over my things. Sometimes, they wore gloves.

Only Buddy knew the real story. Only he saw exactly what occurred that afternoon. Admittedly, I had initial thoughts of vengeance, wishing he had attacked and hurt them. But if he had, he might have been injured or even killed in the process. We knew they had a crowbar, and they easily could have carried a knife or even a gun. If they were bold enough to break a door and come in during broad daylight, I doubt they would have hesitated to hurt a dog.

I squeezed Buddy's neck a little tighter at that thought, pulling him in close and whispering again, "I'm so glad they didn't hurt you."

Silver Necklace with a Circle Charm with Fingerprint Engravings

Although fingerprints have been used since ancient times, modern fingerprints for identification and forensic purposes began in the late nineteenth century in England. Sir Francis Galton developed the earliest classification system based on grouping the patterns into arches, loops, and whorls. The U.S. Federal Bureau of Investigation recognizes eight different types of fingerprint patterns: radial loop, ulnar loop, double loop, central pocket loop, plain arch, tented arch, plain whorl, and accidental.

Fingerprints are formed before birth due to both genetic and environmental factors in utero. No two people have the same combination of patterns, and a person's fingerprint will be the same throughout his or her life.

chapter 20

2012, Littleton, Colorado

I sat on the family room couch in the spot I'd occupied nearly every day over the past few weeks. The cushion indentation matched the curve of my backside and never found its way back to fluff. A low hum from the television produced ambient noise in the room. Baby paraphernalia cluttered the rest of the couch. A small stack of diapers leaned against a box of wipes, and burp cloths and blankets were piled high atop a nursing pillow. The couch's "stain-proof" microfiber suede revealed several constellations of small white stains from spilled milk and the occasional spit-up.

Closing my eyes and sinking back, I enjoyed a moment of rare stillness. I reached for my necklace and grasped the charm between the pads of my fingers, feeling the unevenness in the silver. The grooves and edges engraved on the charm reminded me of the monumental life change that had occurred two months earlier.

Fingerprints, on their own merit, held inconsequential relevance in my life prior to that time. There were a few remnants preserved in my preschool artwork that sat at the bottom of my hope chest in the attic. Fingerprints on those pages were transformed into flower petals or ladybug dots. As an adult, fingerprints played a role in identification, for travel or medical documents, or to open a phone's locked screen. When I worked as a public defender, criminal investigations almost always included mention of fingerprints, and I spent many a cross-examination drilling into this kind of evidence. But I never considered the sentimental value of fingerprints until this piece of jewelry changed that perspective.

Cal was an excellent sleeper and eater, which is all that matters in that first year. But the toddler era revealed his strong-willed personality. His temper tantrums registered on the Richter scale, and his impulsivity often got all of us in trouble. But those aquamarine eyes and fits of wild laughter had a way of turning even the strongest-willed person into a puddle. His curiosity for all things—from trees to trucks to bugs to balloons to airplanes to animals—helped rekindle a sense of wonder in me as I began looking at those same things with fresh eyes, eyes untainted by cynicism or familiarity. Marvel tends to diminish over a lifetime, and kids offer a reboot.

I threw my whole self into motherhood in the same way I threw my whole self into everything, cramming all the Mommy & Me classes our schedule could allow—music, gym, swimming, library, stroller exercise, playgroups at the park, all the while knowing that if we had more kids, these opportunities might not be available.

At age thirty-five, a woman is designated AMA (advanced maternal age), a label that felt like a stab even if it related only to the age of my reproductive organs. Ted and I decided to "not try" to have another baby the same way we did the first time, but it didn't take long to realize that baby number two might be more stubborn.

We began the old-fashioned way. I went off the pill, and we started paying closer attention to ovulation cycles. But month after month, test after test, the results came back negative. I started on Clomid, a fertility drug, and even left a work conference to come home early because we had a window and an ovulation test that gave me a smiley face, a result that meant go time. It took many long and anxiety-ridden months, but finally (finally!), one day, I peed on a stick and saw two lines for the first time since Stone Temple Pilots played in Denver. I told Ted right away. I told everyone right away. Cal was more of a dream than a specific plan, but this time, we worked hard for that extra line.

On a Thursday morning in September 2011, I miscarried.

One day, I was pregnant, and the next day, I wasn't.

Time doesn't dictate the level of heartbreak. A loss is a loss is a loss, no matter where it lands in a gestation period. There's no certain day or week that divides the line between "this is too soon to be considered a loss" and "this is a true loss now." Nor is there a dividing line between who has permission to grieve this kind of loss and who doesn't.

I went to the doctor, and she confirmed what I already believed to be true. Trying to stifle tears, I muttered, "It shouldn't be this sad. It was so early."

"It's okay to cry." She put her hand on my arm. "It's okay to be sad. As soon as you see that test, you commit. It is real."

I had committed. The promise of a second baby had been real. Dreams and plans began the moment that extra line on the stick appeared.

But an upending can take place in a matter of moments.

She softened her voice and spoke to me as a mother, not as a physician. "You need to grieve. Give yourself the time."

I should have heeded her advice and taken at least the rest of the day to feel the feelings and cry. Instead, I went to my friend's birthday party that same evening with a group of women and tried stuffing the miscarriage down deep, pretending like it didn't happen, and distracting myself with other people and their future-oriented plans.

Gathered around a long wooden table in the upstairs room of a sushi restaurant, I blended in with the noise of other people's stories and laughter, not wanting to mention the loss that night so as not to bring gloom into the room or take any attention off the birthday girl. I put on my well-practiced game face and made every effort to avoid my thoughts. While we were eating, my friend stood up for a toast. Even though it was her birthday, she lovingly spoke about each woman present at that dinner and what each woman meant to her. After she rounded the table, she closed with the words: "I want to thank you all so much for coming to this dinner. I thought this would be the time to share some big news with you."

She paused.

She didn't have to pause.

"I'm pregnant!" she shouted, while everyone threw their hands in the air and cheered. Someone squealed an "I knew it!"

On the outside, I celebrated with everyone and took my turn to hug and congratulate her. On the inside, though, I retreated into myself and my sadness. Of course, I felt genuine excitement for her, but her news colored mine in deep bittersweet hues. It turned my loss into more of a defeat. The one had nothing to do with the other, and yet, I held both pain and joy in my hands at the same time.

Fertility challenges are cruel. They create a wicked shame spiral. I assumed, as many women assume, that my inability to conceive and the miscarriage were the results of my failures and a betrayal of my family and myself.

It is difficult to speak something only in whispers. "These are private matters," people say. "Private things should stay private." And yet, this kind of pain pierces like any other pain, often worse than any other pain. My heart broke every two weeks, every one-line test, and every waiting period we endured before we could try again. Every time I spotted blood on my underwear and every time I heard someone talk about her "whoops baby" or that "he only had to look at me and I'd get pregnant," I recoiled, feeling helpless and angry. Every time I remembered the miscarriage or the two lines that became one, I missed the baby who never came to be. I knew I'd miss that baby for the rest of my life.

Deep calls to deep at the roar of your waterfalls.

In February 2012, twins showed up on the sonogram screen.

When the technician pointed out the two barely visible, grainy splotches, Ted sighed heavily, quickly followed by a matter-of-fact "I knew it." He could not have known it.

A hundred thoughts crammed for space in my head as I stared at that image. Two little boys. Or two little girls. Or one of each. The shock of twins quickly gave way to the realization of God's double portion. He gave Cal two sidecars instead of one. The diamonds to the sapphire.

Things were going to get crazy. But I had time to prepare for the crazy. I could handle two babies. After all, I had two hands.

Throughout the pregnancy, people (sometimes complete strangers) made comments like, *You're having twins!? How exciting! Are they natural?*

Natural? Of course, they're natural. They are two human beings, not robots or aliens.

The "Are they natural?" question is really a smokescreen for: Did I have any "help" (fertility meds, intervention, etc.), or did I do this totally "on my own?" (without fertility meds, intervention, etc.). As if my children would be less than if I had "help." As if it would make me less of a mother, as if science and God are always opposing forces. As if these babies wouldn't count as the miracles they are. As if God had no hand in their lives.

Throughout my life, I put up weak defenses in the face

of shame. However, I refused to accept the stigma and shame attached to infertility. It is both unfair and dangerous. I talked to women who struggled for years with heartache and guilt over infertility, and these conversations are always hush-hush with the admonition "Please don't tell anyone this but . . ."

The suffering is real. The hardship is real. The heartbreak cycle is real. The Herculean efforts to conceive and maintain a pregnancy are real. I am, and my children are, real.

Because of my age (thirty-five) and the twins, I needed more monitoring and prenatal visits. These extra appointments soothed my nerves, so I had no complaints about the additional scans. At thirteen weeks, we went for an ultrasound, and as the tech pointed out various parts of "Baby A" and "Baby B," I asked the question.

"How early can you tell the gender of the babies?"

As the words came out, I regretted my impatience. Surely, it was too early.

"Let's take a look and see," she said. My heart lurched so quickly that it felt as if it lifted my chest up and off the exam bed. I almost stopped her from the reveal. I didn't come prepared for this information, but my curiosity jumped ahead of my senses. Ted leaned forward.

"Baby A is a girl . . . and . . . Baby B . . . . looks like a girl too."

Ted and I looked at each other. His eyes resembled planets.

"Are you sure?" I asked the tech.

"Pretty sure!" She pointed to the areas on the screen that convinced her, tiny white splotches of confirmation.

"If you had to put a percentage on your certainty, what would you say?" Ted asked. The absurd but entirely Ted-esque question made me laugh aloud, but I also didn't shut it down either.

"I'd say 85 percent." Her tone matched the conviction in her answer.

85 percent sounded definitive to me, especially when the source of that information is someone who performs ultrasound examinations all day, every day, and is paid for accuracy.

She printed out a couple of the photos and left them on the bed's end before exiting. I slowly stood up from the table, wiping the goop off my belly, trying to assimilate this big new information. Ted said twin girls would be the poetic justice he deserved for all the hearts he broke in his 20s.

"I knew it," he said. He didn't know it.

As soon as the tech pronounced girls, the vision of two curly-haired girls sitting at a small white wooden table took form in my mind. I sat with them in a tiny chair, my knees inches from my nose, handing the girls crayons as they colored on white paper. This scene, and so many similar scenes, created a story of a future ahead. The imagination works fast. We discussed names and nursery design. I bought a few onesies. We told our baby girl news to 85 percent of the world. How could we not? It was 85 percent!

A month later, we went back to the perinatologist for another check-up. I hoisted myself onto the exam table and lifted my shirt as the technician (a different one on this day) squeezed a bottle, and a cold glob spewed out onto my stomach. She moved the wand back and forth, and the computer screen showed the black-and-white pixels that only took shape with explanation.

"Still two girls in there?" I asked, half-joking.

"*Hmm*, let's see," she said.

"Here's Baby A . . . *hmm* . . . nope . . . Baby A is definitely not a girl."

"Wait what?" Propping up on my elbows, I looked at Ted. The two planets appeared for the second time, and he straightened himself in his chair.

"What about Baby B?" he asked.

She moved the wand to the other side of my stomach. "Okay. Let's see . . . here we go . . . Baby B is also a boy."

"Are you kidding?" I whispered. She had to be kidding. "Last month, the person who did the ultrasound said they were two girls. She told us she was 85 percent sure they were girls."

"Not sure why she would have given you a percentage," the tech replied. "It was a little too early in the pregnancy to identify the gender. See," she pointed to two dots on the screen, "we can't deny those."

It wouldn't be the last time a couple of penises derailed my plans.

Author Brené Brown once said, "Grief is the loss of expectation," and this loss of expectation caused me to tear up at that precise moment in the room. I had committed to twin girls in my mind and now had to reel in the line and cast anew.

Not that I loved those two babies any less or wanted to change a single thing about them. I knew they were perfect, but I grieved the loss of the story I created about them.

That's why grief makes us feel so untethered—because we lose the narrative we imagined, the narrative we counted on to play out as we thought it would.

Pivots can be tough, but we still need to pivot. So we did, and by the time we made it to the car, I had a new story of a soon-to-be mom of three boys.

Throughout this pregnancy, I grappled with fear and worry, in part because the twins made it a higher risk but also because this pregnancy came on the heels of such a long period of waiting muddled with disappointment and crushed hopes. The fear of losing the twins to miscarriage made me hold my breath every month during the ultrasounds, waiting for a confirmation of heartbeats. But the exams gave us no cause for concern, and the boys continued growing and developing on course.

Although their due date was October 14, our doctor said multiples rarely make it full term because it poses a danger to the mother. The babies are "fully cooked" ahead of forty weeks. I expected the boys to come a few weeks early, but I wished only for them to come in September because so many people in our family have August birthdays—my mom, dad, Ted, father-in-law, sister-in-law, niece, and nephew, among them. An October delivery might be far-fetched, but September birthdays could differentiate them, and twins can use all the differentiation they can get. As the end of August approached, I prayed fervently for them to simply click into September for their arrival; even September 1 would work.

Instead, they came late in the night on August 31, only hours shy of September, squealing, "Mom! Stop trying to control the narrative!"

Cooper Terry and Crosby Webb both weighed around 4 ½ pounds. Terry, after Ted's mom's maiden name, and Webb, after my mom's maiden name. Cooper came out four minutes ahead of his brother and will cling to this seniority for the rest of his life. After a quick hello, the nurses whisked them away to the NICU. Crosby resembled a purple grape, and the medical team—worried about his breathing—immediately went to work on him. A crowd filled the room during the birth, but everyone left with the boys, including Ted. I still had to deliver the placentas, which took more time than the births and proved to be the worst pain of the entire process. The doctor pressed down on my abdomen with heavy force. Despite all those extra prenatal check-ups, no one had ever mentioned that part.

Eventually, whatever needed to come out came out and left me empty of all signs of the two lives I had carried for months and the hope I had carried for years. A nurse pushed me in a wheelchair down to the NICU to see them. The boys were swaddled with striped baby blankets and donned the same hospital hats that Cal (and every other newborn) wore. Their NICU room housed the two incubators, along with a couch and a lazy-boy chair. The boys had their separate stand-alone incubator apartments with placards indicating their names and birthdates. Nodes and wires covered their bodies, and the extent of mechanisms necessary to keep them alive both marveled and terrified me. I was only inches away from their little bodies, but the clear wall of the incubator's hood seemed impossible to breach. I desperately wanted to hold them.

The nurse helped me to an oversized chair, lifted each baby out of their beds, and brought them to me. Because they were so tiny, I could cradle both boys, side-by-side, in the crook of one arm.

"Miracle A and Miracle B," I whispered over them and closed my eyes. "Thank you, God."

Cooper graduated from the NICU ten days after his birth, persistently first at all things. Crosby waited a few more weeks because of certain breathing issues the doctor wanted resolved before he went home. Those weeks in which I had a toddler and a newborn at home and a newborn in the NICU blurred together and prevented me from being fully present anywhere. Thoughts of the babies preoccupied me when I was with Cal. Thoughts of Cal sidetracked me when I was with the babies. At the hospital, I felt guilty for not spending enough time there, or guilty for leaving the other boys at home. I arrived later than I wanted to arrive and left earlier than I wanted to leave. Ted went back to work immediately after the boys were born, so that did not help either.

A day simply did not have enough hours.

After Crosby finally came home, I had all three boys under one roof, within sight and arm's reach. We created a central headquarters in our family room, with the babies' bassinettes parked at either end of our L-shaped couch. I set up camp on a spot in between the two, surrounded by stacks of baby trappings.

Cal thankfully attended preschool three mornings a week, so in the rare moments when the babies simultaneously slept, I'd take a quick shower or change clothes. Trying to breastfeed two babies made it virtually impossible to do anything else because I had to alternate the breast and the bottle with each baby and afterward pump to try to get more milk for the next round. In the beginning, I tried sticking with breastfeeding, but after three months, I surrendered to formula. Newborns are supposed to eat every three hours, but the whole process and clean-up took almost three hours. I couldn't sustain it, so I simply added the non-breastfeeding guilt to the pile.

I parented like playing a game of whack-a-mole, and I pounced a second too late every time. Many nights, staring up at the ceiling, unable to fall asleep, I made promises to God.

Tomorrow, I'll be the kind of mom I always thought I'd be.

Tomorrow, I'll start fresh and begin anew.

Today didn't go the way I planned, but tomorrow I'll be better.

I screwed things up today, but I will do a good job tomorrow.

One afternoon, when the twins were a few months old, I took all three boys to an indoor jungle gym. Cal, a potty trainee, still needed help in the bathroom. I held the twins, one in each arm, while standing inside the stall door, telling Cal what he needed to do with toilet paper while trying to balance the twins against my body. Other moms came in and out, steering their kids by the shoulders. One woman walked behind me, assessed my situation, and exclaimed, "You are amazing!"

"Thanks," I said.

What I wanted to say is, "Lady, we could use some help here . . . Can you hold one of these babies?"

Amazing is the wrong word. I'd never characterize anything I did as amazing, only simply what anyone would do, enough to get us through the moment and into the next, through the day and into the next.

I wondered if I'd ever look back on these days and call them the best of times like my mom did when she recounted her early motherhood years. Rose-colored glasses and hindsight would help highlight the good moments and fade the not-so-good. Maybe one night, instead of feeling guilty, I'd feel assured and confident drifting off to sleep.

Today, you were the mom no one else could be.

Today, you did the best you could.

Today, you did a great job.

Later that year, my talented friend Alisa custom-made a necklace for me. It had a long silver chain and a round brushed silver charm. Using metal clay, Alisa gathered my kids' fingerprints and then etched the images onto the charm.

From a distance, the charm appeared to have a wavy and textured design, but a closer inspection revealed the definitive markings of fingerprints. Three compilations of arches, whorls, and loops, three one-of-a-kind smudges.

Each fingerprint has a unique design and assignment, as each child has a unique design and assignment. The necklace reminded me that the boys were meant to be exactly *who*, how, and when they were meant to be—matchless in every way. They were meant to be Calvin, Cooper, and Crosby—before I knew them, before I knew to dream of them.

But more than that, the necklace reminded me of the gift that came on the other side of the waiting, the heartache, and the loss.

Gifts can come on the other side of such things.

chapter 21

January 21, 2022

I let go of Buddy, stood, and turned my attention back to the closet floor. I rolled up belts, organized them in one of the emptied baskets, and started placing things back onto the shelves. Buddy, disinterested in my efforts as soon as they had nothing to do with him, sauntered back to the family room.

All day long, I had been imagining what had happened here—what these intruders looked like, how they got into my house, and what they did when they were inside. I couldn't shake this overwhelming desire for the details. I tried to picture them as real people with real voices, trying to get into their heads, to create one story so all the competing storylines would dim:

"Let's just sit and wait," he said as he shifted the car's gear into park.

"It'd better not be long," she said. "It's cold outside. You might need to keep the car running."

"We'll give it fifteen minutes," he said, handing her a sandwich. "See those landscapers from next door on their lunch break? We'll blend right in."

She pulled her hat down to her eyebrows and slumped lower into the seat. "I'm not so sure."

"No cameras, no alarm sign. This should be quick and easy," he said.

They waited and watched as they took rehearsed bites of food and feigned conversation. The snowfall turned light and then stopped as the last flakes settled onto the ground. He clicked the windshield wiper to off, and the blades made their final descent, resting in their assigned slots. They watched the landscapers laugh as they alternated between swigs from their thermoses and drags of their cigarettes.

"Wait, is that the garage door?" She leaned forward toward the dashboard.

He leaned forward too. "Yes. It's opening. Look, only one car in there. Someone must be gone. That's a good sign." He squinted his eyes. "Wait, someone is coming out. What's she doing?"

"Is she shoveling? Oh no. This is going to take too long." She slouched in the seat. "We should go before someone notices us," she continued, already pulling her seatbelt across her chest. "It's the middle of the day. We can't take a chance."

"Wait," he put his hand up in the air. "She doesn't look dressed for shoveling. Those aren't snow boots."

They watched as the woman moved quickly back and forth across the driveway. She almost slipped a few times on the ice. A large brown dog followed her out to the driveway. He tried to eat the snow she flung in the air on the edges near the grass.

"That's their dog! Are you kidding?" she exclaimed. "No way. I'm out. It's huge."

"Hold on," he muttered. "Give it a second."

"Let's go," she said. "I don't want to wait her out. Someone's gonna notice us. Too risky. We can come back another day."

One of the landscapers walked into the yard and started petting the dog.

He smiled. "Look at that. It looks like a nice dog. I don't think it will be a problem."

They stared as she walked up the driveway and leaned the shovel next to the side of the house. He clapped his hands together one time. "She's finished. See, I knew this would be quick."

They saw the woman disappear into the garage, and the dog followed her inside. Twenty seconds later, the SUV's brake lights lit up the dark space.

He sat up straight. "She's backing out right now! She must be leaving."

The car reversed onto the driveway and into the street. The white backup lights flicked off as the car proceeded forward. The garage door slowly came down and closed.

"She's gone," he said. "This is our chance." He put his beanie hat on and slid gloves onto his hands. "Is the coast clear?"

"I don't see anyone out except the landscapers. They won't notice us. But I'm still not sure about that dog. You know how I hate dogs. Remember last time?"

"Let's give it a try and see how it goes. We have options." He opened the glovebox, grabbed a gun, and slid it into his pocket. "Now or never," he added and picked up an iron crowbar from the backseat floor, slipped it inside his coat, and then zipped the coat up to his neck to conceal it.

She buttoned her own coat and pulled on gloves. "Okay. If you say so. But if there's any issue, we're bailing." She grabbed the messenger bag and a clipboard.

They exited the car and started up the street toward the house. They walked to the front door and rang the doorbell. Just in case.

They had a view of the front room through the window and saw the dog on a large pet bed on the floor. At the sound of the bell, the dog turned its head and stared at them for a few seconds but quickly lost interest and slumped back down onto the bed. They looked at each other.

"I think we're good to go," he said, turning for the backyard. She followed on his heels. As they walked, he pointed at the side of the house while she pretended to write notes on her clipboard. No fences in this neighborhood made the job a cakewalk.

As they circled the property, they scoped out the best entrance spot.

"There's the bedroom door," she said, peering inside the glass. "I can see the closet from here."

"Bingo," he said. He pulled the door to see if it was open. "Damn. That would have been a gift." He stuck the end of the bar into the frame near the lock plate and pushed. The frame bowed and forced the plate through the wood. Fragments of the door frame ripped off. It took less than five seconds. He gave her a quick glance and a nod.

They stepped inside and went straight toward the closet.

"Wow." She flipped open the messenger bag flap and swept her gloved hand across the shelf, collecting all the stray jewelry and pouring it into the bag's opening. He started pulling out drawers.

"Nice," he said as he held up a watch, then tossed it into the bag.

She raked through the handbags on the shelves and pulled a couple down. "Here," she said and handed him a backpack. "Use this."

He started at the top shelf, yanking things down, opening boxes, and throwing things aside. "Metal and stones," he reminded her.

She picked up the dishes and emptied their contents into her bag. He pawed through the pajamas, flinging them out as he moved through the piles, running his gloved fingers along the lines of the corners. He pulled the jewelry drawer out with such force that it broke the hinge, and the drawer crashed and fell on his foot.

"Dammit," he swore, writhing as he grabbed his foot with his hand.

"You okay?" she asked. "We need to keep moving."

Clack, clack, clack.

They both froze and looked at each other. He put his hand inside his pocket.

The dog walked into the closet, stood, and looked at them. No one moved, and they stared at each other.

"Hi there," he said and reached out an open palm. The dog took another step and started sniffing the glove. "Good boy," he reached further and started petting the dog's head. He saw the name on the collar—Buddy.

"Hi, Buddy," he said. The dog's tail started wagging at the sound of his name, and they both let out a sigh of relief.

"Come here, Buddy," he said as he walked out of the closet and toward the bedroom door, beckoning the dog with an open palm. He passed the threshold, and the dog followed him.

"Good boy," he said, once the dog stood in the hallway. He then turned and went back into the bedroom, closed the bedroom door behind him, and returned to the closet.

She stood there holding a small safe. "Look what I found."

"Jackpot," he said. He placed the box on the ground and slammed the crowbar on it several times. Then he took the edge of the crowbar and slid it in underneath the door. He stepped on the safe and bent the door until the lock broke.

"Great safe," he murmured. They both picked through the documents and passports and tossed them on the ground when they discovered jewelry pouches. "Remember when you wanted to leave?" he sneered, as he held up a diamond ring. "Would you look at this?"

Her eyes widened, and she beamed. "Okay, you told me so."

They emptied several other rings from the little bags. She then grabbed their bag, and he put the backpack on his back. He slid the crowbar back into his zipped-up jacket. On the way out, they stopped at the bedside tables and opened those drawers. They scooped handfuls of items, threw some things in the bags, and dumped the rest on the floor.

"Let's go," she said. "We got plenty. Who knows when she's coming back."

They stepped over the pieces of the broken doorframe and walked out onto the patio. She pulled out her clipboard, and they slowly walked around the other side of the house, pointing and talking to each other.

They continued the act until they made it back to their car, which was still warm.

"That's a new record for us, even with the dog interruption," she said, glancing at her watch, as they both slid into their seats, and he turned on the car. They pulled off from the curb and drove away.

I opened my eyes and tried to reorient myself and set aside an imagination on overdrive. Despite how vivid the story played out in my mind, it was still just a story, fabricated to serve some unconscious purpose.

Maybe I wanted the story to portray these people as people, not cartoonish villains. Trying to imagine people who had families or debts or desperation, I considered the circumstances that led them to my house. If I could see them clearly and understand their motives, it might relieve my anger and bitterness toward them.

I contemplated what might have been going on in their heads as they sifted through my things, wondering whether they had done it before or if multiple burglaries had made them calloused to any kind of fallout. How did they justify their actions? Did they think we wouldn't miss these things or that this kind of a loss wouldn't matter to us? They probably agreed with all the people who tried consoling us that it was "just stuff" and we should be grateful. We had enough stuff, so we could afford to lose some.

Did they have second thoughts as they drove away? Or, as they started sorting the stash, did they ever consider reversing their course of action? Did it ever occur to them to make things right?

I wonder if I wanted a story so I could imagine them stopping, even for the slightest moment, to contemplate the things they held in their hands, to think about how very much these items would be missed.

Gold Necklace with a Flower Millefiori Charm

Millefiori is a glassmaking technique that produces distinctive decorative patterns. The term "millefiori" is a combination of the Italian words "mille" (thousand) and "fiori" (flowers). Artisans use heat to fuse glass rods of various colors to craft a millefiori object. Next, they slice the rods cross-sectionally to produce tiny mosaics and arrange these pieces into patterns, which are then joined using heat. The result is a unique, intricate, floral glasswork design that resembles a vivid field of a thousand flowers.

The millefiori craft has roots in Ancient Egypt and Rome. Jewelry makers first used the technique in Italy in the fifteenth century, and eventually, millefiori became popular throughout Europe.

chapter 22

1995, Paris, France

Aunt Jenn and I wandered around surprisingly quiet and scarce Paris streets, which provided welcome relief from the crowded tourist attractions that had filled our past few days.

Flowerboxes hung off window edges above the retail shops in one narrow alley while bright green ivy climbed up the walls. Red and blue awnings and umbrellas provided shelter for the occasional person or couple sipping espresso and smoking cigarettes. We browsed the windows of boutiques interspersed among boulangeries and cafes. The windows displayed a variety of things such as antiques, fine arts, vintage clothing, and artisan jewelry.

I carefully watched each step in my Sperry topsiders, trying not to trip on the bulging stones squeezed out of place after centuries of use. My long *Laura Ashley* floral skirt swished with every movement. I wanted so badly to blend in with the Parisians' style and sophistication, but I lacked both style and sophistication, so that made it hard.

As we passed a jewelry store, I spotted a gold necklace with a circular charm in one of the windows.

"I love that one." I pointed to it.

"Let's go look inside," Jenn said as she pushed the door open and walked into the tiny shop. I followed her through.

With a combination of a few basic French phrases and

hand gestures, Jenn asked the clerk to see the necklace. The charm had a flower mosaic pattern with pale yellow and light blue colors. A "millefiori," the clerk said.

"Millefiori," we both repeated.

"I love it," I said.

"Why don't I buy it for you then?" Jenn offered, pulling out her wallet. "It's a gift for you to always remember this trip."

She handed the clerk several paper bills.

"Merci," she placed them into a cash box and handed back some change.

Jenn helped clasp the chain behind my neck before we left the shop. I reached up to the charm and pulled it down, so it settled right below the collar of my cardigan. The clerk handed me an antique mirror reminiscent of the one in *Snow White.* The millefiori pattern of flowers looked different at such a close distance. The colors took on depth, and new intricacies gave the design more dimension.

Jenn is my dad's younger sister, my godmother, and an unfailing presence in my life. She never married or had kids of her own, so she embraced her nieces and nephews. She took me for manicures and shopping and museum visits. I chose her as my sponsor for my Confirmation in eighth grade and my driver for school dances. She worked in sales and spent her days in between airports, every week in a different city, and as a result, she racked up legendary frequent flyer status. She loved Europe, especially France, so she cashed in those miles and offered this Paris trip as a gift for my high school graduation.

We landed at Charles de Gaulle airport in the afternoon. Jenn managed to hail us a taxi and engage in a four-second exchange in French before we headed to our hotel. My heavy, jet-lagged eyes widened at the sight of the Eiffel Tower in the distance.

"Look," I whispered to her, tapping on my window and pointing toward the icon.

We checked into the hotel and climbed up the two flights of stairs to our tiny room, which had two twin beds inches from each other and inches from the opposite walls. The bathroom couldn't have been bigger than a phone booth, yet it somehow contained a shower, toilet, and pedestal sink.

"It's kind of tight in here," I said, scooting around the bed to try to wedge my suitcase in the corner.

"It's kind of French in here," Jenn laughed.

After a quick nap, we walked down to the street to find something to eat. I couldn't believe how many people crowded the streets at nine at night. The cafes we passed were filled with people seated at all the tables, smoking and drinking coffee.

We found a hole-in-the-wall restaurant where I rediscovered my love for croissants.

Over the next six days, I managed to work croissants into every meal. But I wasn't exclusive to them. Baguettes, brioche, boule. Bring on *le pain*. I fell in love with the cheese and every kind of pastry we tried, especially crepes and beignets. I even gave escargot a try.

Jenn planned the perfect Paris adventure, every day a new must-do.

I stood on the bridge in the Giverny Gardens where Monet painted his famous Water Lilies. We rode to the top of the Eiffel Tower for a 360-degree view of the city. Honestly, the *Mona Lisa* at the Louvre let me down a little. As the most famous painting in the world, I didn't expect it to be so small and beige. The stained glass at Notre Dame, however, more than made up for it with its grandeur and vibrancy. I would have taken more pictures had I known that twenty-four years later, I'd watch the majestic cathedral go up in flames on live television, a mishap that took five years to repair.

In the hilltop village of Montmartre, we visited the Sacre-Coeur Basilica, called "the big white church," visible from many other key spots in the city. We met an artist named Hans and bought one of his paintings of an eleventh-century church called *Eglise Saint Pierre de Murs-Erigne*. When the sun momentarily slipped out behind the clouds, we found a park bench in one of the countless gardens and ate sandwiches. The flowers were almost as beautiful as the people. Almost.

"Do people really dress like this in the middle of a Tuesday?" I asked. "They belong on a runway instead of a sidewalk."

I lived in the suburbs of a city less than 140 years old. Paris had existed for over two thousand years; its streets were the same streets in history books and timeless literature.

In the Hall of Mirrors in Versailles, I spun around in circles. "It's crazy to think that a king lived and ruled here and walked these hallways three hundred years ago." I gazed at the ceiling, mesmerized by the gold, the artwork, and the crystal chandeliers.

"Hard to imagine, isn't it?" Jenn said.

"I can't believe I'm here."

Before that trip, my only kind of "travel" consisted of summer road trips to Missouri—my adventures rarely strayed far off the I-70 corridor. My family's western exodus from St. Louis did not mean we never looked back. We absolutely looked back. In fact, we went back every summer of my childhood.

We piled into our minivan for a fifteen-hour trek across Colorado and Kansas to the sweltering St. Louis heat. These trips predated iPads and car TVs, so to pass the time, we brought road trip activities like magnetic board games and Mad Libs. Those things never ate into any significant amount of time, so I spent hours staring at cornfields and battling motion sickness, though my parents didn't call it that. I had my own name—the cramped feeling in the back of the minivan. Generally, the road trips were dull and uneventful, and the only exciting moments included mirages of water on the horizon, gas station stops, and the occasional midwestern downpour. No place does hail like Kansas.

One summer, we encountered one of the worst thunderstorms I can remember. The darkness loomed ahead in a thick shade of charcoal grey. We either drove into that storm or that storm drove into us, but suddenly, hefty balls of ice battered the car with such force I thought they might shatter our windows on their way to pummel us. The windshield wipers whipped back and forth at a dizzying pace, unable to keep up with the deluge. The deafening sound of hail hitting the car reverberated in my bones. It felt like we had driven into a drainpipe, and someone had lit a bunch of firecrackers.

"Michael, pull over," my mom ordered. Whenever she used our full names, we knew she meant business.

"I think that might be worse than driving through it," he yelled, though we could barely hear his voice over the rain's drumming.

"We're going to spin out and crash. Pull over!" Mom yelled back, gripping the handle above the window with her right hand and bracing herself with her left palm pressed into the glove compartment door. My dad edged over to the shoulder of the road and placed the car in park. The hail beat down with such force that I wondered how our van remained upright.

"Everybody get down on the floor and cover your heads!" Mom shrieked.

Tucking myself in a ball in between the second and third rows, my forearms squeezed the sides of my face so tightly my elbows touched. I smelled a combination of shoe dirt, fear, and remnants of Famous Amos cookies. But the storm's roar overwhelmed all my other senses. The five of us crammed into spaces between the seats like pieces in a Tetris game. We waited in silence, our voices no match for the chorus of a thousand banging hammers pounding outside the car.

A few minutes later (though it felt like hours in my head), the hail smacking deescalated and softened into a heavy rain. The car stilled as the rage outside simmered. The storm charged down the highway, finished with us. We stayed on the car carpet, tucked in together.

"Okay, it's over. Everybody back into their seats and buckle up," my dad said.

We crawled into our spots and pulled onto the highway to continue our voyage. No one said a word—the storm had said plenty. When we reached the edge of the rain, the excitement of the storm passed with it and the familiar fields and flatness reoccupied our views.

Every July of my childhood, we drove through those familiar fields and flatness and the occasional ferocious rain. But every single time we exited I-70 onto the St. Louis streets, a familiar eagerness surged inside of me. Stoplights signaled an end to the monotony of the minivan, and we knew we'd soon see my grandma and grandpa. My grandparents only had a rough estimation of our arrival time based on a pay phone call from our last stop. But, without fail, my grandpa opened his front door the exact moment we pulled into the driveway. I bet he stood and stared out his front window for hours, waiting for us. My grandma stepped out on his heels, usually with a camera in her hand. I slid the car door open, jumped out, and with hurried steps, crossed the razor-cut grass, up the concrete walk to the porch, and into their arms.

My grandpa helped unload while my grandma started pulling out an array of food and drinks. Within minutes she had bread, deli meat, and cheese out on the counter, offering to make us sandwiches, always sandwiches. She loved a spread of any kind. I scoured her refrigerator for one of my favorite drinks she stocked up for our trip—the little barrel "juices" with the foil top. She had plastic straws at the ready for us to poke into that foil and suck down a few of those orange, red, and purple elixirs I believed only existed in St. Louis.

"What can I make you?" Grandma asked while she dashed around the kitchen, already in the middle of making things.

"What do you need? How about a sandwich? Something to drink? Maybe some cookies? Frank—grab the cookies. Here, sweetie, have a seat," she said, as she pulled out one of the barstools and patted it with her hand—beckoning to me to sit down. "Let me make you a snack."

Despite the last two days of exclusively sitting and eating, my grandma wouldn't let us refuse her hospitality. But after only an hour, my mom started to get antsy. "Okay, time to go see Granny and Gramps," she said as she popped up from the couch.

So we piled back into the van and drove the two minutes down the road to see my mom's parents. We entered through the front door, exchanged hugs, and assumed seats in the family room on the couch or the braided jute floor rug.

"How was the drive?"

"How is your summer?"

"What grade are you going into next year?"

I answered variations of these questions throughout the week as we reconnected with family members scattered across town.

This is how we traveled. A couch tour around St. Louis.

Sometimes, we left the couches for outings such as a Cardinals game or a visit to Busch Gardens. We made time for the Ted Drewes frozen custard stand where the lines stretched into the streets, no matter the day, time, or weather. Every visit included a backyard pool party and a photo of all the cousins lined up in order of age, often with matching home-sewn outfits. The adults sat in circles in lawn chairs under a metal carport roof. An uncle or two tended the grill and added to a tower of burgers and hot dogs on an oval melamine platter. We spent all day in and out of inflatable pool toys and taking turns on a very stiff diving board.

We packed as many visits, conversations, and midwestern comfort food into our week as possible until it came time to reload the minivan and head back west to Colorado. We hugged everyone goodbye and settled in for a longer drive because it lacked the anticipation of the way there.

The familiarity of the St. Louis trips contrasted vividly with the newness of the Paris adventure. As different as these travels were, I don't think I could appreciate one without the other. St. Louis brought us back to our roots. The Paris trip opened me up to the world. St. Louis linked me to my past and the familiar; Paris linked me to a different culture and ethos. Both collections of memories are part of the unique pattern of my experiences. Both are different blossoms in a field of a thousand flowers. Tiny pieces fused into a beautiful design.

chapter 23

January 21, 2022

How did I let this happen? This question surfaced and resurfaced over the day like bubbles in carbonated water.

Things like that didn't happen here.

Because things like that didn't happen here, I safely assumed they wouldn't happen to me.

Assume and *presume* both mean to take something as true. But to presume something means one has evidence or reasonable proof to back it up. To assume something lacks such supporting evidence.

Things like that didn't happen here.

We rarely locked our doors and never worried someone might break into our home. Our town had a dedicated police force that patrolled the streets and gave notices for open garage doors. Everyone waved to everyone else. Kids played basketball on friends' driveways and jumped on trampolines in their backyards. Everyone knew each other's birthdays and travel plans, and they helped assemble furniture and move it when it came time for something new.

Crimes scarcely occurred in this quiet suburban community. Only on rare occasions did we hear reports of smashed car windows, but that hadn't happened in years. Neighbors looked out for neighbors. But with the advent of doorbell and garage cameras, neighbors did not have to be home to look out for neighbors. When a dog went missing or a brazen coyote strolled down the street in broad daylight, and especially when both events transpired at the same time, calls and group text messages lit up phone screens.

Does the "almost" lack of crime constitute enough evidence to excuse me from blame and justify my inaction when it came to protecting my home? A lack of track record is nothing. Just because things like that hadn't happened before, it doesn't eliminate the possibility that things like that could happen here.

To say things like that didn't happen here is arrogant and ignorant. To say things like that didn't happen here ignores obvious privilege. To say things like that didn't happen here is an assumption without reasonable proof.

Because things like that *did* happen here. They just did.

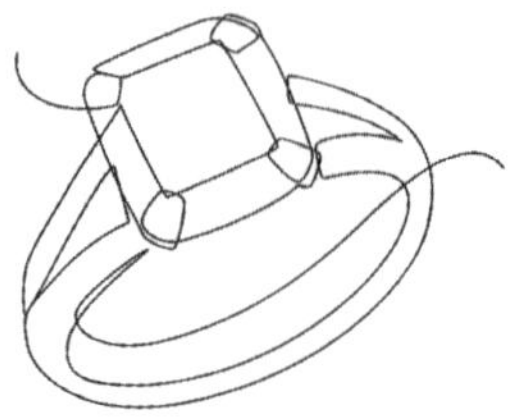

Platinum Ring with a Princess-Cut Diamond

Diamonds are the hardest naturally occurring material and are rated 10 on the Mohs scale of hardness; they are stones that could scratch all other stones. Diamonds are formed deep under the earth's surface with the help of high temperatures and extreme pressure. Diamonds reach the surface with rising magma in volcanic eruptions, only to find their way into hiding again under rocks or rivers via lava.

The word diamond is derived from the Greek word "adamas," which means "unbreakable" or "invincible." Consequently, diamonds have been thought to protect from illness and bolster strength, victory, and courage. The De Beers Corporation is responsible for the perceived market value of the stone, and the company's slogan, "A diamond is forever," launched a boom in diamond sales.

chapter 24

2011, Highlands Ranch, Colorado

"I'm on my way home. Grab Cal. We need to go over to your parents' house."

Ted never came home from work in the middle of the afternoon.

"Your mom called. She wants us to go over to her house because she has some news."

I stood at the kitchen sink, rinsing dishes with my phone propped up on my shoulder. I put the plate down, turned off the water, grabbed the phone with my hand, and held it firmly.

"What? What do you mean?"

"I don't know. She didn't say. She only said to come over as soon as possible."

"Did something bad happen? Is everything okay? Something wrong with my dad?" Pinballs of worry darted around in my head.

"I don't know," Ted repeated. "I'm ten minutes away."

Something had to be wrong. My mom never minced words, and she didn't love surprises. Plus, I spoke to her on the phone every day, often multiple times a day, and I had even spoken to her that morning, and she said nothing of significance. She would never have shared something with Ted before sharing it with me.

We drove to my parents' house in silence. Cal, only two years old at the time, stayed quiet in the backseat, undoubtedly picking up on our anxiety. The clamor continued in my mind.

Adam answered the front door, and we poured into the family room. Mom sat on one side of an L-shaped couch, and Adam resumed his spot on the other side. My heart sank at the sight of my mom's strained face and puffy eyes.

"What's wrong?" I stood in the middle of the room. "Where's Dad?"

"He's fine. I spoke to him earlier today. He's in Salt Lake City for work, but he's taking a flight home. He'll be home in a couple of hours."

We took our places in the same room where we gathered to open Christmas presents and watch football games. The television mounted on the wall above the fireplace hung a smidge too high, so we had to tilt our heads back to watch. After a while, we stopped noticing the odd angle. Cal learned to both crawl and walk in that family room and we changed his clothes and diapers on that carpet. As a baby, he giggled for hours on his back, kicking his arms and legs in the air while he watched the ceiling fan spin high above him. Framed family photographs lined the shelves and covered the walls.

On any other day, I loved the windows that spanned two floors and the bright light and warmth they allowed to fill the room. But on that afternoon, the light shone with such intensity that I had to squint, and the room felt stifling hot. Flicks of dust meandered in the air.

Cal remained uncharacteristically calm and quiet. He went right away to the closet where my mom kept his toys, grabbed some cars, and brought them back to the floor. I moved closer to Cal, and Ted sat in a chair to my right. My mom leaned forward.

We waited.

She looked so small.

In the moment before she said any words, everything was still okay. Nothing had changed yet.

She cleared her throat and took a deep breath. On the exhale, she spoke.

"I'm sick. I have cancer. And it's bad."

Cancer.

"Cancer?"

No.

"Yes."

The earth's plates shifted.

She proceeded to tell us what she knew, a few details, but the details left us with more questions than answers. We asked her about the prognosis, the doctors, and the plan. Everyone repeated some variant of the phrase "one day at a time."

Surgery first. Chemotherapy to follow. One day at a time. The cancer had advanced but not to the point of no return. No one spoke with optimism, but no one called it hopeless. No one said the word "terminal."

"Okay," I said, though it wasn't.

We all stood up and came together in the middle of the room, wrapped our arms around my mom, and locked in.

"One day at a time," she said.

"One day at a time," we agreed.

Ovarian cancer is called the silent killer because its symptoms can be nonspecific and easily explained away by other conditions. Several signs like bloating, cramping, and constipation are things women experience with such regularity that they'd rarely be considered life-threatening. It's only when the symptoms become too significant that they can no longer be ignored or rationalized, and this can mean the cancer has reached an advanced stage.

My mom had her first symptoms one year before the diagnosis. She felt a protrusion in her abdomen but believed it to be what she described as "parts moving around and falling" from getting older but experienced no pain and thus had no serious concerns. In June 2011, she noticed her stomach had started to grow. But still, she didn't worry because "this happens to women in their 60s."

Over the following months, things started to change and symptoms that had been written off as "normal" or "expected" could no longer be explained as such. She felt extremely full and bloated throughout the day, yet she still experienced hunger. And her stomach continued to grow.

She went to the doctor for an ultrasound. Her regular doctor was not in that day, so she saw another physician in the same practice. While she sat waiting in the exam room, dressed in a paper blue hospital gown and reclined on a bed covered in white table paper, she overheard him speaking to a nurse in the hallway outside her door.

"She's not even my patient. How am I supposed to tell her she has ovarian cancer?"

I hated knowing this, that she learned of her diagnosis in a low-pitched and aggravated tone on the other side of a door.

The next day, an oncologist confirmed the ultrasound results and scheduled surgery for the following week. Nick booked a flight.

The hospital's gynecological wing included oncology and obstetrics. I sat in the same waiting room chair during my mom's surgery that I'd later use while waiting for my doctor appointments during my twin pregnancy. Oncology and prenatal. Sorrows and joys.

Her surgery went according to plan, and the four of us—my dad, Nick, Adam, and me—crammed into a tiny meeting room to debrief with the surgeon, who explained he had removed many tumors, including one the size of a softball. Thankfully, the cancer had not yet reached her lungs, liver, or other major organs, but there were indications of it in the tissues and vessels leading to these organs. Chemotherapy would hopefully kill the remaining cancer cells.

My mom endured nine brutal rounds of chemo over the next four and a half years. Sometimes, she had treatment once a week, sometimes multiple times a week. She experienced a range of side effects, including neuropathy, joint pain, debilitating stomachaches, and others. Some days, she did not have the energy to muster a shower; some days, she failed to make it out of bed. When rash flare-ups occurred, she could not wear undergarments, only the lightest, softest pajamas. Walking into the house from the driveway exhausted her, and she always broke out in sweat. As soon as it started, she had no way to stop it. She left places and parties too early to be unnoticed.

My mom's hair had always been her most identifiable physical attribute and something that helped her stand out in a family with three daughters. At age sixteen, she competed in the Miss Flame contest, a local beauty and talent competition reserved only for redheads. She posed for pictures in a white mini dress and tall white boots, hands clasped together slightly below her waist. She parted her long, scarlet hair down the middle in a ruler-straight line, and soup-can rolled curls tumbled down the sides of her face, landing on her collarbone. When she grew older and discovered highlights, the deep red took on a lighter, strawberry-blonde hue, and she abandoned the middle part for various bangs and bobs.

Chemotherapy caused hair loss within a month of her first treatment. Every day, she found hairs on her pillow and more in the shower drain. For someone who had been identified by her hair for her entire life, it felt like losing a part of herself.

She made an appointment to have her head shaved and buy a wig. I stood behind her while she sat in the stylist's chair wearing a black smock that buttoned around her neck. I leaned in to take one last picture of the two of us in the mirror, and then the stylist went to work, first cutting her hair, and then shaving her head.

"Why don't I start looking for some wig options?" I said, turning around so she wouldn't see me cry.

She bought one and, over the years, added more to her collection, though she hated wearing them. She said they itched and made her hot. She never looked like herself with wigs anyway and preferred a head scarf because the soft material provided much-needed comfort.

My mom lost her hair three separate times over the treatment years. The breaks from chemo allowed her hair to grow a few inches, but then another round took it back. Cancer treatment caused all sorts of vicious cycles within its vicious cycles.

Through it all, my mom rarely complained and did her best to put on a brave face. She continually apologized for making us worry, appreciated everyone's generosity, and never asked for a thing. Her treatments continued until her cancer levels normalized, which allowed her short breaks, the longest being three months, but *break* is the wrong word to describe these times because the side effects worsened. She had to be hospitalized twice due to infections.

Chemotherapy is a beat down. All flow, no ebb. It left my mom physically and mentally depleted, with the next course always waiting around the corner. She started treatment with advanced-stage cancer, so there was never going to be a last round or a bell to ring. She needed to live with it, but this kind of living meant exhaustion and pain as the norm, canceled plans, and days divided into pain pill doses and naps.

One afternoon while my mom rested on the couch, her older sister Jan, who had flown out to Denver for a few weeks, sat near my mom's feet while crocheting a blanket. From across the room, I observed these two sisters together, in each other's orbit as they had been their whole lives. Despite living in different states, they remained connected.

At one point Jan stood up and walked into the kitchen and poured herself a glass of water. When she left the room, my mom lifted her head toward me and whispered, "I wish I had that kind of energy. To be able to stand up and walk into the kitchen." She rested back onto her pillow and closed her eyes.

My mom spent most of her daytime hours on that couch, dozing in a makeshift bed with a white sheet tucked in and around the cushions. The sun streamed in through the family room windows, creating a faint haze. One day, while I sat beside her, she slowly grabbed my hand and spoke so quietly that I had to lean close to her face to make out the words.

"Kimmy, I don't know how much longer I can do this."

Eventually, everything hurt. She stopped eating because it hurt. It hurt to swallow. It hurt to go to the bathroom. Every time I visited her, she looked as if she aged years overnight. She started resembling eighty-three-year-old Granny. Mom described her pain as "eternal" and said she could not remember how it felt to have energy. She wanted to stay in bed all day and all night, and her brain ached when she tried thinking.

"I feel flat," she said, her face pale and expressionless. "Just flat. All the time."

In October 2015, four years after her diagnosis, my mom began her ninth, and what would be her last, round of chemotherapy. She announced this to all of us before she started. "This is it. No more." Her bulging medical file at her oncologist's office required two hands to lift. I accompanied her and my dad to what would be her last doctor's appointment. As we sat together in that cramped room, I stared at the file on the counter.

Pages of notes and next steps. Pages of failed attempts and dashed hopes. Pages of maybe this or maybe that. So many pages of what didn't work.

"I want to stop," she said definitively to the doctor as soon as he sat down in his swivel stool. "No more chemo. No more treatment," she added.

"Okay," he said, without surprise or any hesitation, as if he expected it.

He then looked at me and my dad and said, calmly and matter-of-factly, "Your mom and wife is a VIP around here. She's incredible. She's done everything she could."

"But what about a CT? Is there any way to help her eat? Should we explore alternative treatment plans? Any other new clinical trials?" I grasped at every last straw.

He answered gently. "No."

She did everything she could.

My mom followed, "Last time, you said it would be six to twelve months. I assume the timeline is shorter now?"

My shoulders slumped when I heard those words because I heard in her voice how desperately she wanted him to say the timeline was shorter and her disappointment when he said it had not changed. I saw the defeat on her face.

In that moment, I understood. She did everything she could.

My mom started getting her things in order, wanting to make sure my brothers and I each had something of hers as a keepsake. Adam received an old watch that my mom's dad had given to her. She gave Nick her own watch. She gave me her diamond ring. A beautiful, three-carat princess-cut diamond in a halo setting. This ring replaced my mom's original engagement ring, a gift from my dad for their twenty-fifth wedding anniversary.

He saved up for it for years. Every time I tried it on, I could not imagine wearing, much less owning, something so valuable.

But I could not imagine losing someone so valuable either.

Toward the end of her life, I had many rich and good conversations with my mom, the gift of a long goodbye. Knowing her time was coming, she spoke without reservation.

"I knew long before I decided to quit treatment I was already dying in my mind," she said. "It just took my heart a little while to catch up. In my heart, I wanted more time, the chance to watch my grandsons grow."

My three boys and Nick's two sons were my mom's motivation to keep pursuing treatment, and when she became too weak to engage and play with them, she started to lose the will to keep going. She could barely get out of bed or walk up the stairs, and she certainly couldn't cook or craft with the boys like she loved to do. Her greatest joy felt like work, and when that happened, her heart aligned with her mind.

In January 2016, she decided to begin hospice. Her pain had steadily increased since she stopped treatment. My dad became a full-time caregiver and nurse, organizing and doling out medicine in quantities appropriate for ten people, not one person. He took on the role she had always played for him and for the rest of us. He paced around the kitchen with charts and a pencil, on the phone with the on-call nurse. He continually reached atop the refrigerator for a brown wicker basket containing all the different bottles and foil packs and extra-large plastic M-T-W-TH-F-S-S pill boxes. He reviewed his notebook to double and triple-check the schedule.

My mom vomited all the time. Her medication caused constipation and additional pain and made it difficult for her to go to the bathroom, which then prevented her from eating.

A ruthless rotation. Another vicious cycle within a cycle. She started wasting away.

We took turns at her bedside, bringing cold washcloths and rubbing her hair. Sometimes, she went several days without food, and we believed it to be the end. But then she'd miraculously wake up and feel better, even strong enough to eat some morsels or take a few sips of a milkshake. The swings were difficult to predict and to observe.

She carried an old ice cream tub with a blue handle—the generic ones that contain sherbet or Neapolitan flavors and held it as if it were a purse, being sure to keep it always at the ready. Sometimes, as she sat perfectly still, she'd wince in extreme pain and grip a pillow or the arms of a chair. She could not make it upstairs, so she stopped going there. Then, she couldn't walk across the room, so she only did when absolutely necessary. She barely moved at all anymore.

The vomiting never relented, even after she stopped eating food. She lost weight, and she lost her smile. She stayed in the same pajamas for multiple days in a row. She stopped making sense when she spoke, and she cried all the time. One afternoon, when I sat beside her on the couch, she whispered, "I just want to go to sleep and never wake up again. I just want to pass out."

This was no way to live. No way to die, either.

She began with at-home care and an on-call nurse who visited once a week. Shelly brought a different voice and straightforward conversation. She doled out realistic expectations in a kind and tender way and asked my mom questions like, "Are you scared to die?"

The end closed in on us.

But the last weeks provided some sweet moments.

One afternoon, I crawled into bed with her as she drifted in and out of sleep. I rubbed her head, ran my fingers through her wispy hair, and tried otherwise to keep still. We both lay on our sides, facing each other, so close I felt her breath. The blankets felt so heavy, the pillows so soft.

Those moments were surreal to me, but also eerily familiar, as if I'd been there before, in her bed, staring at her as she slept. Long ago, from a time before I could remember.

She slowly opened her eyes and whispered, "Kimmy, you couldn't have been a better daughter." She paused, and my eyes welled up. "Except for seventh grade." She managed a chuckle, proud of her own joke. I couldn't remember the last time I heard her laugh, and I tried memorizing the sound.

My mom's friends kept watch with us. I brought the boys every time I could and smiled as they sprinted to jump on the bed and fight over who got to be the closest to their Mimi. I spent some time reading aloud to her while she listened with her eyes closed next to me. Every so often, I'd hear a quiet *aww* or muffled giggles, or she grabbed my hand or patted my leg.

With each new day came a new chess game with the medication. Sometimes, what worked one day failed the next. My dad felt inadequate and unprepared; in his words, he was "below average at best." He spoke with Shelly at frequent intervals when Mom's pain escalated beyond the medicine's control. When she finally reached the point that necessitated full-time supervision, I thanked God for giving my mom the ability to make the call herself. She told me separately she didn't want to die at home so my dad would have that memory in what would soon be his, instead of their, home.

In the beginning, we spoke of things in the long term. When we discussed her diagnosis, outlook, and treatment options, we took broad strokes.

If she does this treatment for nine weeks, she should be able to have a break for a couple of months.

She could live for years with this cancer. It's all about keeping it at bay.

I'm going to see how this treatment goes and then decide later.

I'll celebrate when I make it five years.

She came so close to five years.

My heart divided in two. On one side, I yearned to stay in that space where she was still alive. On the other side, I wanted to sprint past the inevitable loss. But, like all things with my mom's cancer, we had to accept the timing as God's alone and move behind my mom's pace.

But we never stopped praying for a miracle.

She rode in an ambulance to the facility and my dad followed in his car. Mom waved as a queen would in the ambulance's back window to all the cars she passed on the road. She probably laughed at herself in there. I sure hope she did.

Her hospice room had some nice comforts, including a quilt on the bed and artwork on the walls. It looked like a hospital room trying not to be a hospital room. Shelly's official role as my mom's in-home hospice nurse ended that afternoon, and the care transferred to the facility staff, including a nurse named Tina, who lovingly cared for my mom and for us during those weeks. I didn't know it then, but Tina would come to be one of the most important people in my life, a kindred spirit and mentor. I never would have thought something so beautiful and important could have its start in a hospice room, but our friendship did.

We began what would be the final vigil.

We took turns and rotated seats. My dad took the business hours, and I came in the evenings. Adam filled in and made sure my dad ate lunch and dinner. Nick joined us from Virginia and Aunt Jan flew out from St. Louis. We all lobbied for the one comfortable chair in the room.

•••••

Before my mom died, I had romantic notions of hospice. Gardens, new-age music, and everyone dressed in white. I thought there'd be narrow paths to follow while pushing my mom in a wheelchair around blooming flowers, gazebos with tables with glass pitchers full of ice water and sliced citrus fruits. I predicted we'd have many bedside conversations, reminiscing over the past and sharing pearls of wisdom.

Turns out hospice isn't so romantic.

We continued taking our turns next to my mom as she slept, waiting for her to die. As a family, we decided we wanted her to be comfortable and peaceful, and we asked for palliative medicine to accomplish this.

The kids came and said their goodbyes. Originally, I planned to have everyone together when the time came, but plans are meant to be held loosely, like the plan for my kids to know their grandma for decades more. As her time in hospice progressed, she looked worse, almost a distorted version of herself. Without any food or drink, she lost body mass at a quickening pace. I wanted the kids to be able to say goodbye, for her to see and hopefully recognize them, and for them to have memories of her as their Mimi, not this diminished version.

Before I brought the boys over to the hospice, I talked to Cal to make sure it was something he wanted to do. The twins were still too young to understand, but Cal knew enough to be given a choice.

We sat at the kitchen table. I looked him in the eyes and said, "Cal, I need to ask you a very important question."

"Okay," he said quietly, a puzzled look on his face.

"Remember our talks about Mimi's cancer? You understand

her cancer is bad right now, and soon she's going to heaven?" He nodded.

"I want to give you a chance to say goodbye to her one last time. It's completely your decision. If you want to go, I'll take you today. But if you want to stay here, that is totally okay with Mimi and me. She knows you love her and you're going to miss her. She looks pretty bad right now because she feels so bad, so that might be tough to see. If you want to go, I'll bring you there and stay with you. If you don't want to go, that's okay too."

I tried to stay calm, but my voice quivered. He dabbed the corners of his eyes with his sweatshirt sleeve, looked down at his lap, and whispered, "No, I want to go and say goodbye."

"Okay. We'll go."

I brought all three kids to my mom's room, and we knocked quietly on the door. She slept on her side. Cal stepped up first. He sat in a chair next to the bed, closest to my mom's head. He leaned in and kissed her forehead. "Hi, Mimi. I love you."

At the sound of his voice, she opened her eyes. She smiled and whispered, in a weak and barely audible voice, "I love you, Cal."

Next, the twins took their turns. Each one crawled up and stood on the chair and said, "I wuv you, Mimi."

I walked down the hall with the boys to the front door. Jan took them back to my house while I stayed behind with my mom. After they left, it occurred to me that my sons had just had their last experiences with their grandma. From that moment on, it would be only memories. Cloudy memories for Cal and supplanted memories for Cooper and Crosby. They were too young.

But everyone was too young. Too young to lose a grandma. Too young to lose a mom. Too young to die.

We continued to watch and wait as her body slowly shut down. She conceded, and we accepted the transfer of suffering from her onto us, as we had to now move into the future without her. And that was going to hurt.

When I was born, Granny sewed a Humpty Dumpty doll for me. I called him Humpy. He consisted of an oblong white pillow stuffed into an outer cover with eyes, nose, and mouth. Thin strips of plaid fabric sewn on the sides served as his arms and legs. According to my mom, I carried Humpy with me everywhere, including to bed every night. All the wear and tear left him bruised and battered. Mom washed him one too many times, and the pillow exploded in the machine. She made a new egg-shaped pillow, but it never fit the outer covering as tight as the original one did, so I carried the pillow around instead. He had no features or limbs, but he was still Humpy. My mom always knew how to fix things, how to make things okay.

Eventually, she thought Humpy would explode if he had another spin in the washing machine, so she resorted to spot-cleaning and attaching duct tape, and I followed with Band-aids to all the wounds and scrapes he received from non-stop play and love. Love hurts sometimes.

There came a day when we simply could not put Humpy back together again. My mom decided it was time for him to go and live with all the other Humpys in a beautiful faraway land called "the Dumpy."

He'd been through too much, and he did everything he could.

At the Dumpy, Humpy could find his Happily Ever After.

The day came and my mom, Humpy, and I waited on our front porch for the man in the big trash truck to take Humpy to the Dumpy. When the trash truck pulled up to our house, we walked slowly to the curb. With crocodile tears on my cheeks, I handed Humpy to him. I asked him if he'd take my Humpy to live at the Dumpy.

This kind man knelt in front of me and looked me in the eyes. He promised me he'd see to it that Humpy made it to his new home and held out his arms. I handed him Humpy, and he lovingly pulled him into his chest, close to his own heart. Then he stood up, turned, and climbed back into the driver's seat. He placed Humpy on the seat next to him. He waved goodbye and drove down the street. My mom and I stood there on the curb, waving goodbye, until the truck vanished around the corner. I was five years old.

Thirty-four years later, I said goodbye to my mom. It was a Sunday morning.

I stayed at the hospice the night before until 9:00 p.m. Adam followed to stay overnight. When I left, she appeared to be sleeping peacefully, though her loud and heavy breathing sounded anything but peaceful. Tina assured us she experienced no pain and that her ear-piercing gurgling sounds did not cause her any discomfort.

I slept fitfully through the night, waking up every twenty minutes to check for updates on my phone, which I kept right next to my pillow. At 7:00 a.m., the sound of my kids trampling around the house jolted me awake and I quickly checked my phone again. Still no news. I made the kids breakfast and went back to the closet to get dressed. But when I came back out to the kitchen, I discovered three missed calls from Adam. He answered on the first ring.

"Mom went downhill rapidly last night, and Tina said if you wanted to be here when it happens, you need to come right away."

I hung up the phone and ran to Ted. "We need to go! We need to go!" I yelled through tears. My heartbeat skyrocketed as I quickly called my friend Jen and handed the phone to Ted, who explained the situation and asked if she would watch the boys.

This news we had expected for so long came and it hit me like a complete surprise. I anticipated this call every day for the previous few weeks, yet I received it as if it came out of nowhere.

When Jen arrived, I ran past her with a quick and tearful thank you. We jumped in the car and left. Despite the sparse Sunday morning traffic, we hit every single red light.

"Come on," I huffed. "You have got to be kidding me." My knees shook.

We pulled into the hospice parking lot, jumped out of the car, and sprinted to her room. Dad, Jan, Nick, and Adam surrounded her bed.

I fell on top of my mom, crying loudly, kissed her forehead, and held her hand. Squeezing my eyes shut as tears pooled up inside them, I knew this day had been coming and had played it out a thousand different ways in my mind, yet none of those narratives prepared me for the real thing. It still shocked me. It still shook me. She was the one who was supposed to fix things, but she couldn't fix this broken thing. None of us could. Only God.

"I love you, Mom. I'm going to miss you."

For a couple of hours, we moved in and out of the room and hallways, waiting. At one point, I told my dad to go in the room and have a few moments alone with Mom. I pulled the door closed and joined everyone in a circle of chairs outside the room. Later, he told me he rubbed my mom's hair and whispered, "Go to heaven, Nancy. You deserve it. I love you."

She saved her final moments for her sweetheart.

Dad opened the door and motioned for all of us to come back inside. Tina put her stethoscope to my mom's heart to listen, and then she looked up and gently said, "She made it."

She made it.

She did everything she could. And she made it.

On February 21, 2016, God stepped down, drew near, held her tightly and lovingly to his heart, and brought her next to him. He promised to see to it that she made it to her new home, to her happily ever after. The rest of us stood and watched her until she was gone, waving goodbye, as she vanished around the corner.

We all surrounded the bed where our mom took her last breath. Her spirit was gone, and only her body remained.

Plates shifted again.

The dullness of death created an immediate staleness and an urgency to leave that building. We shuffled out of the room into the hallway. As I stepped through the doorway, I turned my head for one last look and watched Nick lift the white sheet that had been tucked around her chest and sides and gently pull it over her head. He was the last to walk out of her room and shut the door behind him.

We came home and told the boys. Cal cried. The twins didn't understand, but they picked up enough of our cues to understand that something bad had happened. I sat down and sent an email to a long list of people to share the news, struggling to write the words I'd been planning to say for weeks.

Ted encouraged me to go for a run. With each step, I prayed for a sign, desperately wanting a vision of her sitting on a rock or a bench but would have settled for something less obvious. I looked and listened, willing to "read into" anything that could be interpreted as a sign. But a sign didn't show that day, or in the days that followed. I don't know what I expected, but again, plans and expectations had no play here.

A few weeks later, I sorted through my mom's things. My dad wanted her stuff accounted for and out of their closet. He didn't want the reminders every time he walked in there. We each coped in our own ways. I didn't want this particular job, but I also didn't want anyone else to have it.

I moved my hand along the line of hanging clothes, noticing the varying textiles and colors. The beaded Santa sweater she wore at Christmastime. The electric blue shift dress she wore to my cousin's wedding. A silk blouse that screamed 1990. Maxi skirts from her floral print phase. A gardening bucket hat sat atop a high shelf. Her favorite summer strappy sandals were tucked below a shelf stacked with pajamas. With a deep sigh, I began piling things into boxes.

Wrapping up a life is so sad.

The closet looked so expansive with half of its contents gone, the way a closet looks in the middle of a move. The racks now held only rows of my dad's white, navy, and black shirts and pants; the vibrant colors were all gone. The space looked empty and dull, like a flower bed in winter, missing signs of life.

I set aside some things to send to my aunts and cousins, others to my mom's friends, and donated a few boxes to charity. My friends Laura and Christy benevolently helped me with this process. After clearing the closet, only my mom's purse remained, hanging from a hook on the wall.

On the end of her bed with the purse on my lap, I stared at it for a long time. This one was going to be tough. I slowly unzipped it and dumped the contents on the bed. Receipts of the last things my mom purchased before hospice when she still made purchases. A ticket stub from a Christmas choir performance she attended at her church in December. Half-empty boxes of mints and half-used tubes of Chapstick, appropriate for a life cut off halfway. Wadded up balls of Kleenex, so soft they almost disintegrated in my hand, such a grandma trademark. I reached for her sunglasses, reading glasses, and a notepad with an unfinished to-do list. The sight of her handwriting made tears resurface, and the unfinished to-do list nudged those tears right out.

She finished unfinished.

In one of the purse pockets, I found two vomit bags folded in half, the ones you'd see in an airplane backseat pocket. My poor mom had to carry barf bags in her purse. That is how bad things had become, how sick the cancer made her. I knew death would give her a deserved relief from her suffering, but it wasn't until I held those bags that I accepted it.

My heart had to catch up, I thought, *like she said hers did.*

And for the first time, I considered the reprieve death gave her. We never stopped praying for her complete healing. That prayer had been answered, just not on this side of heaven.

I dug back into the purse one last time to make sure I didn't miss something. In the bottom, where the lining is gathered into a corner, I found a tiny gold angel pin tucked in the fold.

Wedged between my thumb and forefinger, I examined it in the light. The "gold" rusted to gray because of time and the friction of the purse's lining, but a few shiny traces remained, unwilling to tarnish.

I didn't ever find my sign in the sky or on the land. Instead, I found it in the bottom of a purse.

A few months later, I mustered the courage to have my mom's diamond ring sized for my finger. The jeweler looked at it and said, "Wow, what a beautiful ring."

"It was my mom's ring," I quickly replied. "She just died."

I did this all the time with people, including complete strangers, wishing I could wear a sign around my neck that read MY MOM JUST DIED, overwhelmed by the need to let people know, and wanting to say the words out loud because the feelings inside were simply so big they couldn't fit.

My mom's ring never felt like my ring; it felt like hers on loan. The ring connected me to her in a way nothing else did.

On the day I picked it up after it had been resized, I ran into my friend Laura outside the jeweler. She clasped my hand and brought the ring up closer to her face. "That is so beautiful. You should never take it off."

I should never have taken it off.

Instead, I kept it in a tiny leather coin purse inside a pseudo-safe, worried that I'd lose it every time I wore it.

I lost it anyway.

Nothing is truly invincible. Not diamonds. Not moms who have cancer.

One day later that spring, I drove to soccer practice with all three boys in the back of the car when Crosby's high-pitched voice carried above the music.

"Mom, is Mimi walking in the sky on top of us? When can we go to heaven and pick her up?"

Before I could respond, he added, "And Mom, there are no cancers up there, right?"

"Right. That's so very right."

Later that night, I had a dream.

I walked around a vast, coastal, outdoor market. Ted and the boys were there with me. The wooden planks underfoot and the mist in the air reminded me of Seattle, but I couldn't be sure. People crowded the scene; some lined up at booths and food carts, while others strolled, their kids running circles around them. The sun peeked out in a cloud-packed sky. The sounds of lapping water, chirping birds, and garbled conversation reverberated in the air that smelled of fish, saltwater, and funnel fries.

I spotted my mom across the pier. She wore a white shirt, a floral skirt that dropped a few inches below her knees, and sandals—the same outfit she wore the previous Easter. She walked alone, with determination, and upstream of the crowd flow. I only saw her back, but I knew it was her.

I yelled, "There's Mimi!" and started running, shouting, "Mom! Mom!"

I held Crosby's hand, and he kept up with me, though our pace slowed because of his short legs, which required five steps to my one. Ted jogged with Cal and Cooper behind me. I moved as fast as I could, but the swarm of people forced me to swerve and stop several times to allow people to move.

She kept walking, too far away to hear my yells above the commotion around us. I kept an eye on her; her floral skirt made it easier to do so. She ducked inside the front door of what could have been a restaurant; the only clue was a wooden sign hanging above the door, and the words on the sign had been so weathered it made them hard to read. I pushed my way through the flood of unaware strangers as Crosby kept in tandem with me. Ted yelled from behind, "Go ahead, we'll find you!"

We made it to the restaurant and pulled open the door. The substantial size of the inside space surprised me, given the unassuming exterior. Bodies and noise filled the rooms. Every table appeared occupied, and the lobby was jammed with people waiting for seats to open. Distorted voices competed with the hustle and bustle sounds of a restaurant, conversations, and waitstaff hurrying around the room with urgency. I stopped in the middle of the crowd and did a panoramic scan of the room, searching for her.

She sat at the end of the bar, alone, reading a large plastic menu held in her hand. I pushed my way through the tight maze of people and furniture, dragging Crosby along with me. We sashayed past waiters and busboys until we came within ten feet of the bar.

"Mom!" I yelled, though still my voice barely carried over the noise.

She looked up. She heard me.

"Mom!" I yelled again.

She turned and saw me. Her eyes opened wide, and her jaw dropped open.

"Kimmy!" she shouted and jumped down from the barstool and moved toward us.

She dropped onto her knees in front of Crosby and bear-hugged him.

"Mimi, we found you!" he exclaimed.

She cupped his face with both of her hands and kissed his forehead. "Hi, sweet boy." Her voice dropped so low I could only make out the movement of her lips as she whispered in his ear. She must have said something funny because he started laughing. Then she stood up and wrapped her arms around me.

"Mom, you're here. You're here. I've been looking for you for so long."

She turned and picked up Crosby, held him in one arm, and reached out with her other arm to take me back into her embrace. She enveloped us with the same strength she had before cancer. We stood there, in the middle of that packed restaurant, holding onto each other for a long time.

She loosened her grip, pulled back, and studied us for a few moments.

"We have so much to catch up on," she said as she stepped back and returned to her seat. She pulled Crosby onto her lap, patted the stool beside her, and looked up at me.

"Sit here. Tell me everything."

chapter 25

January 21, 2022

I reached down to the floor and grabbed the leather coin purse which held my mom's ring. It had been scattered on the floor along with all the other things in the safe. I checked it one more time, though I'd already opened and closed the pouch twenty times that afternoon, hoping the ring might still be there, and turned the lining inside out as if the ring could have been stuck in the threads and they'd missed it.

Of all the stolen things, losing that ring hurt the most. Not because of its value, but because of what it represented to me, which made it invaluable. Memories of her. Memories of what had to happen for that ring to end up in my possession. Her life. Her death. Losing the ring brought it all back. Loss upon loss upon loss.

Grief is such a small word for such a colossal experience.

Everyone says grief is like ocean waves. Some days, that rang true. Grief does move like water with its fluidity, flux, and precariousness. But grief reminded me more of an electrocardiogram with sharp rises and falls, not the curvature of ocean waves with smooth, gradual crests and receding angles. Grief spiked or plunged more than it arced or retreated.

In the beginning, I barely got through a single day without weeping. When I felt a surge, I'd crawl back to a place in my closet, a corner where I shoved my hanging clothes over to one side. I'd squeeze into that space and tuck my knees up to my chest. I'd go there sometimes to hide, pray, cry, or simply to sit and miss my mom.

On good days, I grieved in this kind of controlled manner.

But it didn't hit me with such convenience every time.

One afternoon at the pool, six months after my mom died, Cooper could not remember where he left his flip-flops, and it set me into a complete tailspin. I marched around the pool deck, searching for them, asked the lifeguards to help me, and even stooped so low to dig into the trashcans, looking for them.

As if he had lost a diamond ring instead of rubber flip-flops.

I finally gave up, packed up our things, and stormed out of there, unraveled and despondent.

Of course, the shoes had nothing to do with it. The loss—and it could have been any kind of loss—hurt because it tapped into the greater grief.

Later that fall, I received a note from my son's teacher that he had misbehaved at school and was sent to the principal's office. It wasn't the first time something like this had happened, but it was the first time that I did not have the chance to ask my mom what to do.

Standing in my kitchen with my phone in my hand, I fumed, not at Cal, but at my mom for leaving me when I needed her help.

I reread this teacher's note over and over, and thoughts raced through my mind as to how to respond. All I wanted to do was call my mom and ask her how to make it all okay. How would anything ever be okay again with her gone?

I looked at my phone and yelled at it as if she were on the other line.

"Mom, why did you have to leave me? I don't know what to do! I'm not doing the right thing, and I need your help. You should be here right now. Why are you gone?"

The words only boomeranged back to me, hitting me in the gut, because she wasn't there to receive them.

These kinds of episodes happened all the time.

Moments of despair in the corner of the closet, complete freak-outs in public, and random spells of anger. And so many urges to pick up the phone and call her, especially every time something significant happened.

Over the years, those grief events decreased in number, but they didn't go away. Life without my mom didn't get easier; it merely became more familiar. Life goes on because life has no other choice but to go on.

But losing her ring unlocked something inside of me. The old emotions overwhelmed me in the same ways they did in the days, weeks, and months after she died. Losing her ring felt like losing her all over again.

I stared at my empty hand.

An urge to call her overwhelmed me, something that hadn't happened in a long time. But her voice in my head still sounded clear and recognizable.

Mom?

Kimmy? You okay? Did something happen?

Mom, I'm so sorry.

What happened? What's wrong?

People broke into our house today.

Oh no! Are you okay? Is everybody okay?

Yes, everybody is okay. They came in through our bedroom door.

Oh no.

Mom, they stole all my jewelry. Your things too. Your diamond ring. I'm so sorry.

Oh, honey, it's okay. The important thing is you're safe and no one got hurt.

Yes, but your ring . . . I was so stupid, Mom. I should have taken better care of it.

It's okay, Kimmy. It's just a ring.

But it's your ring, Mom. You're gone. I have nothing left.

It's okay.

But Mom . . .

It's just a ring. And it's not all you have left.

Thin Gold Chain Necklace

A chain is a series of metal links or rings, connected to or fitted into one another, and used for various purposes.

The chain necklace is one of the earliest forms of jewelry, dating back to ancient times when chains were made with items such as feathers, bones, and shells. The oldest metal chains, consisting of threaded gold and silver, were discovered in royal Egyptian tombs.

The most basic chain is created by soldering each new link closed after it has been passed through the former link. Over time, the chain evolved to incorporate different lengths, thicknesses, and materials, as well as assorted techniques to connect the links. Despite many variations, the basic chain necklace design has retained the same form for thousands of years.

chapter 26

2016, Highlands Ranch, Colorado

I saved Mom's jewelry until the very end, as the last thing to sort through in the wrap-up of her things. A daunting task, even more invasive and wrong than her clothes. But someone had to do it, and again, I didn't trust anyone else to go through the collection piece by piece.

Sixty-three years' worth of jewelry, including a tiny bracelet she wore in her newborn hospital photo and a teal-colored rubber wristband for ovarian cancer awareness. Two bookends of her life.

Chunky gold drop earrings and choker necklaces characteristic of the 90s. Some crystal vintage broaches. Sculptural luxury pieces with mixed metals as well as cheap, decorative things she wore to entertain her fourth-grade students. Expensive 18-carat gold David Yurman bracelets, alongside snowman pins and strings of plastic beads.

I set aside some of the pieces—some for my mom's family members, others for the future. If Adam ever got married, his future wife might appreciate something at their wedding. I imagined handing it to her on the day, maybe as her "something old." Or Adam could end up with a child who might love something from a grandma he or she had never met. Or maybe someday one of my kids or nephews might have a child who would appreciate a multi-generational heirloom.

After organizing the jewelry into piles on my parents' bed, I slid various pieces into mailing envelopes to send to my aunts and cousins. I put the "future" pile into a large Ziploc bag, wrote *Mom—Future* on a note, and stuck it inside. I decided to keep that bag with me until it came time—for all the people we had not yet met. I returned some pieces to the jewelry box to save for another day.

One of those items rested under a white paper square with my mom's handwriting. I picked up the note and traced the letters with my finger. *Mom.* Any evidence of my mom's handwriting became a treasure to me after she died. I lifted a thin gold chain necklace from underneath the paper. It had no pendant or charm.

"This must have belonged to Granny," I said aloud, delighted at the discovery. I didn't have any of Granny's things because she had three daughters, five granddaughters, and one great-granddaughter, so there were too many of us to lay claim on any of her jewelry.

I slid my finger along the chain. Over time, the gold had developed a slight patina that gave it an antique feel. Granny would have found that beautiful.

Mary Poehling met Lilburn Webb when she was only sixteen years old, on a blind date through mutual friends. After serving during World War II, Lilburn reconnected with one of his friends from the Marines back home in St. Louis. This friend brought his girlfriend along, and the girlfriend invited her friend Mary for a double date and what would become the beginning of a burgeoning romance, a romance that unfortunately suffered a blow when Mary's family relocated to Dallas. But Lilburn wouldn't give up; he even worked a series of jobs to help pay for his daily phone calls to Mary, a tenacity that paid off. When Mary's family returned to St. Louis, he proposed.

On July 2, 1949, one day shy of her nineteenth birthday, Lilburn and Mary wed at St. George's church—the same St. George's church where Frank and Ruth Intagliata married and where, later, my parents did. Mary and Lilburn spent only one night in a furnished basement apartment after deciding they did not want to share the small space with thousands of cockroaches. They found another apartment the next day and lived there until their first child, Jan, arrived. Mary's father again transferred for work, so he asked his daughter and her new husband if they wanted to buy the family house for $5,000. They happily accepted the offer, and their next three kids, Nancy, Randy, and Wendy, came in succession over six years.

Lilburn worked nights at a Shell Oil gas station and eventually became the manager. Mary volunteered at the hospital and hosted Tupperware parties in friends' living rooms. She loved the independence and the chance to have the family car to herself for an evening. In the late 70s, she decided to go to nursing school, and for fifteen years, she worked the night shift as a labor and delivery nurse at St. Anthony's Hospital.

My cousin Lori recently discovered old home movie footage. In one clip, the family is sitting around the kitchen table. My mom must have been in her early 20s. She sat on her dad's lap, wrapped her arms around his neck, and squeezed. She flung her head back and screamed, "*I love my dad! I love my dad! I love my dad!*" Everyone in the room laughed, both with and at her. But she kept howling as she professed her love. Gramps didn't say a word, only sat there and beamed.

Granny collected turtle figurines in all sorts of colors and sizes. No one in my family knew why she collected them, only that she did. She displayed her collection on the family room's tiered glass shelving unit. The bottom shelves housed the non-breakable turtles—those she allowed the kids to touch.

The higher shelves, higher but no more than four feet tall, held the glass and porcelain turtles, the "no kids allowed" turtles, which proved a testament of sheer will considering they sat right at kids' eye levels.

Granny had mad yarn skills. She tried teaching me how to crochet so many times, but I didn't have the patience. I started and stopped a thousand projects throughout my life, but lost interest as soon as I noticed a gap or stray thread. Granny crocheted until her dementia prevented her from understanding patterns. Cognitive decline is hazy, but the inability to understand crochet patterns is stark.

Years ago, my mom rediscovered her old diaries in the storage room. We read through them together and laughed until we cried. They had yellow crinkled pages and entries from 1964 through 1968, her preteen and teen years, the prime diary ages. Main themes included love gained and lost and strife with her mother, but there was also plenty of the mundane.

> ***August 14, 1964***: *It was cold today. Randy left for a camping trip. Got two new headbands for 21 cents each and a binder for $1.50.*

> ***August 23, 1964***: *Didn't go swimming. Wendy thinks she has a toothache. Got a root beer at A & W Root Beer. Jan started eating a dog biscuit.*

> ***August 26, 1964***: *Got a coat. Went to Busch Stadium. John asked me to go steady. I refused. Cardinals won 4–2.*

> ***November 17, 1964***: *I like Gary so so much. I'm so shy when I'm around him. Wish I wasn't.*

***November 26, 1964**: It was Thanksgiving. Mom had the dinner. It was delicious. I love the whole world.*

***December 4, 1964**: I'm so SO happy. I don't know why. I suppose I'm getting the Christmas spirit.*

***December 13, 1964**: Forget Gary. Jim is my man.*

***January 9, 1965**: I think I am losing love for Jim.*

***January 11, 1965**: Went back to school. I'm so mad. Mom and Dad don't even trust me to walk to school early. I would have to leave when the bus comes. Tomorrow, I think I will walk up at 8:15.*

***January 23, 1965**: Mom cut my bangs! They are terrible! I'm so mad. I told her not to but she did. They stick straight out. I hate the whole world.*

***January 25, 1965**: Got a new purse. It was $3.50. I'm not too mad now for my bangs.*

***February 9, 1965**: I don't like anybody in our family except the two dogs. Not really. I like everybody. Mom and Dad are trying to teach me things.*

***March 9, 1965**: They always gang up against me. I'm grounded and I can't use the telephone for one week. Not my fault. Jan and me had a fight. She got what she wanted. I got a long bawling out.*

***March 27, 1965**: I really love Mom but sometimes I am so mad at her. I'll always love her, Dad, and the rest of the family.*

April 4, 1965: *I love Mom. She just tries to teach me things when she gets mad. I love everybody (Larry too).*

April 16, 1965: *Danny gave me his ring. I have to keep it hidden. Mom and me getting along good.*

August 15, 1968: *I'm going to develop a whole new philosophy. I'm going to try to be nice to everybody. Maybe that way I'll get a guy. Let's hope so.*

November 15, 1968: *I got my driver's license. I got a 98 on it! My driver's ed teacher is so neat. I luv him!!! Got report cards yesterday. I got all Bs and two Cs. I got a job at Federhoffer's Bakery. I get $1 an hour. It's money!*

My mom's words struck me as reminiscent of my own. As soon as I returned home that afternoon from her house, I headed straight for my hope chest and sifted through yearbooks and letters and sorority paraphernalia until I found my own diaries.

July 27, 1987: *Dear Diary, today Mom got so mad. She said I shouldn't watch tv all summer. So I had to clean my stupid closet ALL DAY!!! Boring! I wonder when I'll see Derek again.* (A lipstick kiss was also applied to this page.)

August 4, 1987: *Today was Mom's birthday. I gave her a card and potpourri. I also begged her to let me have double pierced ears. I'm still hoping.*

August 28, 1987: *I think I might like Ed. He is so nice. He is one boy out of a million that would treat me with some respect.*

September 16, 1987*: Mom grounded me today for the stupidest reason. So now I'm stuck here forever. I'm so mad at her.*

September 18, 1987*: Things have been very different in the past 17 days. Everybody has a boyfriend. And me, I don't know. Diary, I know this is all I ever talk about, but it is the big thing in my life. I like Eddie.*

My diary entries proved there really is nothing new under the sun. The same topics, the same strife, the same cycles of love and loss. These words of my mom not only allowed me a glimpse of her as a daughter, they also revealed the connective tissue in our stories.

For almost thirty years, I had the precious gift of my grandparents. Gramps died first in 2005. His burial took place at Jefferson Barracks, a national cemetery dedicated to veterans. Green rolling hills lined with identical white headstones dating as far back as the Civil War stretched for miles, so uniform and vast they created an optical illusion.

Gun shots rang out and bagpipes played as the family huddled around his casket. Two soldiers slowly and ceremoniously folded the flag draped over it, then clicked back on their heels as one turned and handed it to Granny, who placed it on her lap.

The priest gave a final blessing as he swung a golden ball dangling from a chain and incense smoke surrounded the casket. No one made a sound except the unknowing and interrupting birds, chirping and singing over the priest's words. The birds' melodies contrasted the somber ritual. Two men, dressed in gray coveralls, looked on from afar, ready to get to work after we left the cemetery. A military burial is nothing if not efficient.

At the reception, we took turns at buffet tables lined with enormous serving bowls of iceberg lettuce heavily coated with Italian dressing and foil pans brimming with toasted ravioli, cheese bubbling and marinara sauce crusting in the corners.

I repeated this funeral service three more times, for each of my grandparents after they died. Because Gramps and Grandpa served in the military, they and their wives had designated spots in Jefferson Barracks, and their funeral ceremonies followed the same template. I never once made it through "Taps" without tears.

Granny was the final closed parentheses on the grandparent line of my family tree.

I saw her for the last time at my cousin Sarah's wedding in 2019. At eighty-eight years old and far along in dementia, Granny did not always recognize us and often drifted in and out of sleep. Uncle Randy and Aunt Karen helped her dress for the wedding and wrapped her head with a beautiful scarf for warmth.

As Randy pushed Granny down the aisle in a wheelchair to her designated spot in the front row, she shouted, "Well, hello, everybody!"

Throughout the ceremony, Granny kept shouting "Yay! Yay! Yay!" and other cheers. She stole the show, and my boys pressed their hands over their mouths to stifle their laughter.

My mom would have loved it.

On that day, Granny's behavior reminded me of the video of my mom in Gramps's lap, flinging her head back in laughter and shouting how much she loved her dad.

After the wedding, while we waited for the requisite group photographs with the bride and groom, Granny kept asking Cal to be in every family picture beside her. "I want that one!" she'd say as she pointed to him. He looked so dapper in his little suit; maybe that was what caught her eye, but she certainly locked in on him. My mom would have loved that as well.

Ted, the boys, and I gathered around her before Randy left to take her back home. "It's so good to see you, Granny." We each took a turn hugging her.

It was so good to see her because I knew it would be the final time. I couldn't have curated better last moments as she sat there under a crocheted blanket, words of joy spilling from her mouth.

Granny died in June 2020, three months after the world shut down due to the COVID-19 pandemic. I traveled alone back to the funeral, which mirrored the funerals of my three other grandparents. We all stood around the casket as the priest gave his blessing and swung the incense ball. This time, Aunt Jan accepted the folded flag.

After returning home from the funeral, I put my suitcase down in the kitchen and headed directly to my closet. Using a stool to reach a box on the highest shelf, I grabbed it with both hands and brought it down, careful not to let it slip. I sat down on my closet floor with the jewelry box on my lap. The floral design on the top had faded from all the years the box resided on my mom's dresser due to the steady stream of afternoon sunlight through the window. I brushed my finger back and forth over the flowers, remembering the last time I had opened this box. Right after my mom died, in her room, while I sat on the edge of her bed, sorting her jewelry. I slowly opened it and saw the same gold necklace resting in the corner, under the white piece of paper with my mom's handwriting. *Mom.*

I held the chain high as I set aside the box on the ground, stood up, and walked over to the mirror. After closing the clasp behind my neck, the chain settled on my chest, and the metal felt cold on my skin.

With my hand over the necklace and closed eyes, I imagined my mom and Granny together in a beautiful place somewhere.

Links soldered once again. A field of flowers encircled them, and the sun made their faces glow. They both wore beautiful scarves. They stood, looking at each other for a few moments, and then my mom leaned in, wrapped her arms around her mom in a tight embrace, and whispered in her ear.

"It's so good to see you."

chapter 27

January 21, 2022

I spotted the Ziploc bag in the corner of my closet. No longer sealed, the bag's contents lay scattered on the floor. I picked up the yellow sticky note stuck to the floor next to the bag. *Mom—Future.*

The note and its obvious sentimentality had not deterred these people from stealing what was inside. I sifted through some of the discarded pieces: one gold hoop earring, a cancer ribbon pin, and a chunky chain bracelet.

How could they? I thought, remembering the other items packed in that bag, pieces now gone: a diamond tennis bracelet, gold Yurman earrings, and a dainty antique watch—all the things I set aside for hypothetical future family members. I recalled the day I filled the bag, imagining handing down these items and gifting such important links to my mom.

But now those pieces were gone, leaving me with nothing to give.

I started placing some of the castoff items back into the Ziploc bag but then sat back on my heels and stared at the note. *Mom—Future.*

What if those people never actually come into our family? Adam may never have any kids. I may never have any grandkids. My romanticized scenes of passing down Mom's jewelry may never make their way out of my imagination.

They're stuck there now, I thought. Even if our family grows, the jewelry is gone. Those aspirations will never be more than pipedreams.

That Ziploc bag sat on my closet shelf for six years. It would have stayed there decades longer. I should have given all of it away to the people who were alive. At least my mom's things would still be in the family because they wouldn't have been in my closet during the burglary.

More protective of an unknown future than the known present, I took a risk and lost.

Jewelry isn't meant to rust in a Ziploc bag.

Or in a box.

Or in a safe.

I should have given more of it away or at least worn the things I had more often.

But I always worried I might lose them and, if that happened, someone might join our family, and I'd have nothing of my mom to give. This need to keep these pieces of my mom stemmed from a self-appointment as a guardian of a future that never came to be. We all ended up losing.

My fears did me no service, as fears rarely do. I reached over, picked up the empty Ziploc bag, held it in my hands, and examined my palms through the transparent plastic film.

I stared at the swirls and loops on my finger pads, the wrinkles on the inside of my palms, and the veins that spanned the heels of my hands. The freckle below my left thumb had been there since childhood. I don't think I had ever looked so closely at my hands as through the filter of that empty bag.

I stared at the tattoo on the inside of my wrist, my mom's signature traced from my birth certificate. Staring at my empty hands, I realized the impermanence of it all.

I counted on and trusted *things*. But things can't be counted on or trusted because they don't last forever. They are always eventually going to disappoint. If not me, then someone after me.

If I wanted to secure a piece of my mom to pass down in the future, I needed a better option.

I stood up, walked across the room, and threw the empty Ziploc bag in the trash.

Coral Flower Stud Earrings

Coral: a color composed of pink and orange tones, symbolizing warmth and acceptance, evoking an upbeat spirit.

chapter 28

2018, Silverthorne, Colorado

One summer afternoon, my friend Lindsay and I roamed around a Banana Republic. I waded through a pile of clearance items and pulled out a cardboard square with a pair of coral-colored flower stud earrings.

"*Hmm*," I said, contemplating a change from my standard gold studs.

"You'll wear those all the time," Lindsay said, reading my mind and sensing my indecision.

"You think so?" I looked at her. "I'm not sure. It's a pretty bright color. I don't usually do bright colors."

"You'll be surprised. Go for it. Think of them as the 'Lindsay-told-you-so earrings.'"

I laughed. "We'll see about that." I turned and headed toward the cash register.

Turns out, she told me so. Every time I tried those earrings on with a particular outfit, I didn't think they would coordinate. But they always did. Who would have thought an orange and pink combination could harmonize with so many other colors? Whenever I wore the earrings, I thought of Lindsay.

We met seated across from each other at a crowded Mexican restaurant, celebrating our friend Sarah's birthday. Midway through the chips and salsa, I knew I loved Lindsay. She taught high school English, a dream job of mine, and I told her so. She laughed through every other sentence, mostly at herself, and we became fast friends.

Lindsay shared my love of words. She wrote poems and rap songs to honor other people or big events, always finding her way to a rhyme, even if it meant faltering a bit on the rhythm. But nothing ever stopped her from performing, no matter the audience or its size. Unafraid and unabashed, she spoke and sang anywhere and anytime.

She honored others publicly, something that doesn't happen as often as it should. For friends' birthdays, she'd ask us to bring an encouraging note to whatever gathering she had organized, and she brought a decorative box to collect all these notes after we each took turns reading them aloud. Lindsay knew the impact of the gift of words. She did this a couple of times for me, and on tough days, I'd open that box to reread the reminders of love.

But on her own birthday, Lindsay instead prepared notes for the people who came to celebrate *her* and recited those reflections in front of the group. She went down the line and recognized every person with tender specificity. She didn't reserve this kind of thing for only her birthday, however, and that was one of her many brilliances. Lindsay never hesitated to tell other people how much they meant to her, even on the inconsequential days, and sometimes those days were the days we needed the words the most.

Lindsay used her words in creative and encouraging ways, but she also never shied away from difficult conversations. She was determined to say what needed to be said, not what someone wanted to hear, which is a rarity in female friendships. Though we love the yes-women, the truth-tellers are indispensable and important.

Students—past and present—adored Lindsay, a teacher many

would remember as their favorite. She poured her heart into her students, just as she did with her friends and her family.

Our sons were born three months apart, and Lindsay and I navigated those early parenting years, tears, and fears alongside each other. Sometimes, we shared good news, but more often, we laughed and commiserated about things that went wrong. Our friendship did not stop when our kids started outgrowing park play dates; we simply changed scenery.

No one brought more fun than Lindsay did, and she reminded me a lot of Ted in this way. One time, she showed up to a Madonna concert with crimped hair and fishnet stockings while the rest of us wore jeans. Lindsay took every opportunity to showcase her infamous worm move, dance floor or not, and even after the couple times she ended up with a bloody chin. Lindsay brought color to an otherwise black-and-white scene. The coral to our monochrome.

Some people say, "Call me if you need anything." Others simply show up on your doorstep unannounced. Every person needs a first responder, and Lindsay was mine. Like my mom, she fixed things and made things okay. In fact, I also saw a lot of my mom in her, which made her such a safe and comfortable space for me in the tough years after my mom died.

Whenever we had the time, we hiked the beautiful Colorado mountains together. On those trails, we discussed and solved all sorts of problems. Sometimes the world's, and sometimes our own. We made sense of the things that didn't always make sense.

What I wouldn't give for one more of those hikes.

Lindsay lost her life to suicide on September 23, 2021, a week shy of her forty-fifth birthday. I remember exactly where I stood when the phone call came and the feel of my knees hitting the kitchen floor after I received the news. Lindsay's death, unlike my mom's, was entirely unexpected and inexplicable.

With my mom, I spent so many years pre-grieving and getting familiar with the idea that the cancer might take her life. My mom's death was a slow drip; Lindsay's was a lightning bolt.

At her funeral, the church filled beyond its capacity. Despite the COVID-19 pandemic restrictions on indoor gatherings, people packed in rows and stood in the aisles. Thousands of faces were fixed in bewilderment and deep sadness. Lindsay's daughter sang bravely, making everyone crumble when we heard her tiny voice amplified in the auditorium. Her son spoke of Lindsay as a wonderful mother. Her brother spoke of her humor. Her colleagues spoke of her fearlessness. Her father spoke of her in heaven.

The next day, friends and family gathered in a beautiful outdoor space by the Platte River. The invitation said to wear bright colors to match Lindsay's spirit. The grassy area glimmered a deep emerald hue. Gorgeous wildflowers with all the colors of the rainbow scattered the surrounding field, even some in the coral color of those earrings I bought with Lindsay years before.

The sunshine warmed our cold aches. This party resembled Lindsay—casual and communal, the stories and speeches felt like a slide show on repeat. People spoke of her influence and inspiration. They told funny anecdotes. Her daughter sang another song. Tears intermingled with laughter. The entire day had a buoyancy that reminded me of Lindsay. She smiled on us that afternoon, from a place far away, a place even more brilliant than that space by the river. We all hugged each other for a few beats longer that day. I said, "I just can't believe it," more times than I wanted to count.

But I couldn't believe it.

No one could believe it.

Without saying goodbye, I slipped out of the party early and on my own. I walked toward the parking lot and saw Lindsay's husband talking to his mom, away from the crowd. They stood far enough away not to notice me. I continued down the path toward my car, quickly slipped into the driver's seat, and turned the key. The radio blasted a song, but I hit the power button and turned it off. I simply sat there in the quiet, my hands on the steering wheel, and stared straight ahead of me without focusing on anything, looking at nothing.

I thought of that magician's trick of yanking a tablecloth out from a fully set table while everything stays in the exact same position. For Lindsay's family, everything flew up in the air but landed on the ground, shattered. This was no trick.

Back in 2016, in the days leading up to my mom's funeral, I prepared to give the eulogy. The importance of this task weighed on me. No one else had planned on speaking, so I wanted to make my words perfect to honor my mom's memory. I wrote and practiced the speech many times in my family room, with Ted as my only audience. On the night before the service, I asked Lindsay to come over to hear it. Lindsay, who always championed my writing, also served as my go-to editor and constructive critic. Because she said the things that needed to be said, I knew she'd be straightforward with feedback, and I trusted her with what would be the most important speech of my life.

She sat on a corner of my family room couch, and I stood at the opposite corner of the room and practiced the speech. I looked in a different direction because presenting a eulogy to one person felt awkward, so I spoke to my kitchen appliances instead. Lindsay had a pad of paper and a pen on her lap. After a deep breath, I began.

"Before my mom died, I asked her what she imagined heaven would be like. She told me her favorite description of it—one she heard at another funeral she attended years ago.

'When a person dies, she boards a sailboat. On the shoreline stand all the people she's leaving behind. Those people are crying and hugging and waving goodbye. As the boat pushes off to sea, she watches and cries, too, waving goodbye to everyone left on the shoreline. Soon, the people will be lost in the distance.

'But in a short time, she sees another coast, in the direction toward where the boat is moving. She moves to the front to watch as the boat approaches the new shoreline. Slowly, slowly, it comes into view, and she sees a different row of people on that beach. These are the people who came before her. The family and friends. They are all there—waving, laughing, cheering, and hugging each other—welcoming her home.'"

My mom described this version of death and heaven to me a few months before she died, and it seemed like the perfect way to open a eulogy. The image of her being welcomed on that beach brought comfort and joy to my spirit, and I hoped it would do the same for others.

After finishing the speech in the family room, I looked over at Lindsay. She sat back against the couch cushion and let out a long breath as she handed me her notepad. On the top line, she wrote "The Parable of Immortality."

"I'm stunned," she said. "The description your mom gave of heaven is my favorite as well. It is based on an old poem."

I had no idea this story originated from an actual poem, but when I researched it, of course Lindsay was right. What an outlandish coincidence that these two important people in my life both loved this relatively unknown poem.

When Lindsay died five years later, the coincidence became providence.

I glanced in my rearview mirror and noticed that Lindsay's husband and mother-in-law no longer stood in the parking lot, and I guessed they had likely returned to the gathering. Exhaling a long breath and resting my forehead on top of the steering wheel, I thought of "The Parable of Immortality." I grabbed my phone, did a quick internet search, and reread the poem as I sat there, the tears I'd kept locked down for the last few days now streaming down my cheeks.

> I am standing upon the seashore.
> A ship at my side spreads her white sails to the
> morning breeze
> and starts for the blue ocean.
>
> She is an object of beauty and strength,
> and I stand and watch until at last she hangs
> like a speck of white cloud
> just where the sea and sky come down to mingle with
> each other.
> Then someone at my side says,
> "There she goes!"
>
> *Gone where?*
>
> Gone from my sight . . . that is all.
>
> She is just as large in mast and hull and spar
> as she was when she left my side
> and just as able to bear her load of living freight
> to the place of destination.
>
> Her diminished size is in me, not in her.
> And just at the moment
> when someone at my side says,
> *"There she goes!"*
> there are other eyes watching her coming . . .
> and other voices ready to take up the glad shout . . .

"Here she comes!"

And that is dying.

I pictured Lindsay on a ship as the rest of us waved goodbye on the shore.

There she goes.

Then I thought of my mom waiting on the other beach along with the crowd, cheering as Lindsay arrived.

Here she comes.

Yellow African Beaded Bracelet

chapter 29

January 21, 2022

Crosby walked into the closet.

"Cros, I can't right now," I said, assuming he needed me to do something for him. He didn't answer, and when I looked at his face, I noticed he wasn't looking at me. Instead, he surveyed the scene, scanning the piles on the floor.

"You looking for something, Cros?"

He didn't answer and gingerly stepped forward into the closet's corner.

"Crosby, be careful. Don't come in here. Don't step on . . ."

"Yes!" he exclaimed, ignoring me.

He reached down and grabbed something off the floor and then held it out for me to see.

A bright lemon-yellow bangle bracelet rested in his hand, a gift he had given me the previous Christmas. One of the teachers at his elementary school volunteered in the summers at an orphanage in Uganda. Every year, she returned with beaded jewelry and tchotchkes to sell at a fundraiser called the "African Bead Store" at school. This event strategically took place in early December so kids could do some Christmas shopping. Every year, I gave the boys some money to buy something, and they habitually chose colorful wire-beaded animals to add to their safari collections. Last time, however, Crosby used his money to buy me a bright yellow bracelet as a gift. He knew I loved the color yellow.

Crosby stretched out his arm, offering the bracelet to me.

"They didn't take this one," he smiled.

I lifted the bracelet from his palm, and he turned and walked out of the closet without another word.

Staring at the yellow bangle as I ran my fingers over the beads, I turned it round and round before sliding it onto my wrist.

They didn't take this one.

His words nudged something inside of me.

As I had so many times that day, I surveyed the closet, looking for missing items. Although the thieves indiscriminately swept handfuls of jewelry to steal, they also discarded things without obvious value.

Like this yellow bangle Crosby gave me.

I stood up, suddenly energized. After hours of searching for what was gone, I looked at the piles with different eyes, searching instead for what remained.

I picked up three rainbow stretch bracelets that my friend Sarah gave me for my birthday one year and tucked those bracelets behind Crosby's bangle on my wrist. An antique watch dangled off the shelf, almost as if it couldn't decide if it wanted to jump. The watch didn't work, and the tiny face was so scratched I could barely make out the numbers. It looked like something you'd see under the costume jewelry counter at Goodwill. But the watch belonged to my grandma, so I'd held onto it all these years. I slid the watch onto my other wrist.

A teal beaded necklace lay curled on itself on the floor. I wore that necklace to my mom's funeral in honor of ovarian cancer awareness. I clasped the necklace around my neck and put on one of the newly single dangling glass crystal earrings from my wedding day in an earlobe. The crystal had yellowed over the years, but it still caught the light and made a faint prism on the wall. My mom and I chose those earrings because they resembled the lace of my dress.

A beaded gold bracelet encircled my right wrist, and a tiny gold disc engraved with the letter *L* dangled from one of the beads. Alisa, the same person who made my fingerprint necklace, designed these bracelets for some of Lindsay's friends after she died. I didn't wear it all the time, but I had fortunately worn it to lunch earlier that day.

I walked over and stood in front of my full-length mirror, appreciating these beautiful things, and realizing that all is never lost. Even when a lot of it is.

WHAT REMAINED

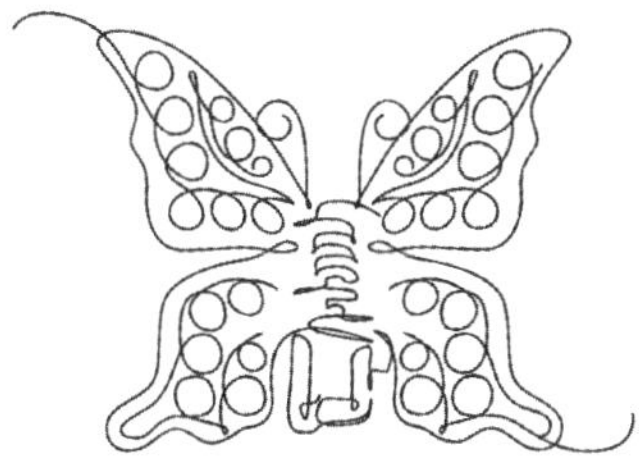

Butterfly Hair Clip with Silver Rhinestones

Long Cream-colored
Beaded Necklace with a Geode Charm

Thin Yellow Leather Bracelet

chapter 30

2013, Littleton, Colorado

When Cal was four years old, my mom took him to the Dollar Tree to shop for my birthday. She told him he could pick whatever he wanted. He walked up and down every aisle, down and up again, deliberating this monumental choice. My mom, always so patient and long-suffering, allowed him to go at his own pace.

After more time than should ever be spent in the Dollar Tree, Cal decided on a butterfly hair clip. He called it the "most beautiful thing he had ever seen." My mom bought it and helped him with the gift wrap. He handed the present to me with great expectation and delight.

"Cal spent hours shopping for the perfect present for you, and he chose this." Mom winked.

I opened it slowly, enjoying his anticipation. He stood as close to me and the gift as possible, not wanting to miss the big reveal. Just like another time, long ago, I stood beside my mom as she opened a dazzling butterfly.

As the wrapping paper dropped to the ground, I smiled and lifted the butterfly clip high for everyone to see.

"Oh, Cal!" I exclaimed. "I love this so much. How did you find it?"

"Mimi took me to the store, and I picked it," Cal said, grinning with pride. "Do you see all the diamonds?"

"I sure do. It's so valuable. I've never seen something so pretty." I swooped him into a bear hug.

I unfastened the butterfly from the cardboard square and immediately clipped it into my hair.

"You did such a good job. Thank you for this beautiful gift," I whispered into his ear. "It's my favorite."

"See Mimi"—he turned to my mom—"I knew it."

She squeezed his arm. "Yes, you sure did. You made a great choice."

He strutted across the room with profound satisfaction and resumed playing with his toys on the carpet, clearly uninterested in the rest of the party.

My mom leaned over and said in a hushed voice, "Cal really deliberated over his choice. He took it so seriously."

"Thank you. I love it, and I'll never forget it."

I hadn't thought of it until that night in the closet. The butterfly clip rested in one of the open boxes on the floor. I picked it up and tipped it back and forth to see if the closet's overhead light caught the rhinestones.

The sparkling wings transported me back to that birthday, and I could picture my young son clearly as he stood beside my knees while I unwrapped his gift. I could also imagine my mom walking with him down the aisles of the Dollar Tree while he searched for it.

At face value, this butterfly clip resembled a cheap piece of plastic with acrylic rhinestones glued to it.

The story behind it made it so much more.

2016, Littleton, Colorado

Three days after my mom died, my friend Sarah showed up on my doorstep. I saw her standing through the front window, and when she spotted me, she smiled and waved.

"Hi," I said, opening the door, surprised to see her.

She stepped inside and hugged me. "I'm not staying. I only wanted to stop by and give you something." She handed me a small box, wrapped with a bow.

"What is this? You didn't have to bring me a gift."

"It's really nothing. Just a little love."

I tugged at the bow and opened the box. Inside, a long chain of ivory beads with a two-inch geode charm was coiled inside the box atop a white fluffy square. The geode was a mixture of gray and sage colors, and a thin gold lacquer line formed the border.

"This is so beautiful," I said, holding it in the air.

"I thought rather than flowers or food, I'd give you something you can always have, something to remember you are loved whenever you feel sad." I lifted the necklace over my neck, clasped my arms around her, and whispered, "Thank you."

She was right about the necklace. Every time I wore it, I thought of her and that day when she brought me love.

The geode stuck out of one of the piles on the closet floor. I pinched the charm with two fingers and unearthed the necklace; the dangling beads hung in the air as I lifted it. The stone felt smooth, and I ran my fingers up and down the beads in the same way I used to do with my rosary. Staring at the mix of colors in the geode, I realized I never had looked close enough to notice the thin cracks in the stone.

Love can have cracks and still be lovely.

I stood up in front of the closet mirror and slipped the necklace over my neck in the same way I did that day with

Sarah. She moved to Texas years ago, and though I hadn't seen her in a long time, I never forgot the love she gave me on that day. I was grateful to hold it again in the face of this loss.

I'll borrow the love from that day for this one, I thought.

Love works like that. It can traverse multiple losses.

2017, Moshi, Africa

In 2017, I bought a bracelet embossed with the words *Be still and know,* a reference to the verse from Psalm 46:10. *Be still, and know that I am God.*

The mustard-colored, thin leather band had a gold clasp. I loved this psalm and had read and heard it a thousand times, but I had never really considered the words in a meaningful way. Nevertheless, I put that bracelet on and never took it off, even for exercise or in the shower, which is not the best way to care for leather, but it did make it soft, pliable, and inconspicuous around my wrist. After wearing it for so long, I didn't notice it, the same way people might stop noticing their wedding rings after never taking them off for years. I had grown so accustomed to the feeling of the band around my wrist that I forgot it was there, and I certainly never thought about the words.

That changed on a mountain in Africa.

On October 6, 2017, Ted and I summitted Mt. Kilimanjaro in Tanzania. At 19,341 feet, "Kili" is the highest free-standing mountain in the world and the tallest peak in Africa. We trekked it for six days and five nights and encountered hot and freezing temperatures, food poisoning, and the effects of extreme altitude.

Camping at night proved to be as great a challenge as the climb. The only person who hated it more than me was Ted.

Zip. Zip. Zip, zip, zip. Zip. Ziiip. Zip.

The sound of the zipper opening and closing the tent's inner and outer doors became part of the trip's soundtrack. During those cold nights, I crossed my legs and willed myself not to have to go the bathroom at 3:00 a.m., which, of course, had the opposite effect and only amplified the need. Scrounging around in the dark for my headlamp and puffy coat, I crawled over to the tent door, and *zip, zip, ziiip, zip, zip, zip, zipped.* After a visit to the shrubs in the dark, I stumbled back to the tent to do the whole thing in reverse. *Zip, ziiip, zip.* A universal camping experience, the sound is hardly specific to that mountain, but I hear the *zip* in my head every time I think of that trek.

Our little group became a family on that trail. Over those million steps, we covered every topic imaginable. The climb itself was not challenging or technical, but the length and time required to finish demanded grit. We passed through five climate zones. On the first day, we walked on a narrow trail covered by a canopy of tall green trees, and a few days later, we walked on volcanic rock resembling the moon's surface.

Despite the challenges—the monotony of one step in front of another and sharing a tiny tent with Ted for five nights among them—the prize of the summit eclipsed all other things. Nothing compared to standing on top of the world. Located on the Kimbo volcanic rim, Uhuru Peak is the highest point on Kilimanjaro. There stands a sign made from wood planks reading:

> Mount Kilimanjaro
> Congratulations
> You are now at
> Uhuru Peak, Tanzania 5895M/19341FT Amsl
> Africa's highest Point
> World's Highest Free-Standing Mountain
> One of the World's Largest Volcanoes
> World Heritage and Wonder of Africa

Uhuru means *freedom* in Swahili, commemorating the freedom Tanzania celebrated from British colonial rule.

Over so many days, even with six people, there comes a point of conversation fatigue. Except with Ted. He never fatigues. But when things got quiet or when voices swirled around me without requiring my participation, I savored it, often preferring to be on the edges of conversations, not inside of them.

We spent time in silence, listening to the air and the sound of gravel beneath our footsteps. In those moments, I walked alone with my thoughts, bending my fingers over that yellow bracelet, brushing the smooth leather, and repeating the words inside my head. *Be still, and know that I am God.* My body moved, but my mind settled. After all those months of wearing the bracelet, I never really thought about the words on it until that hike.

Peace came easier to me on that mountain. No phone, no news, no updates. My fingers moved in a horizontal motion across the band. *Be still.* Breathe in. *And know.* Breathe out. The clouds dropped so low that they created a foggy haze. We walked across the sky.

I thought of my mom, of the past eighteen months, the ick of grief that still coated my insides. I didn't ask for the grief to go away because the grief is what kept me close to her; I only asked for peace and stillness and to sit in the love and the lament.

On the summit day, we moved at an excruciatingly slow pace. A full second between every single step. "*Pole pole,*" our guides said repeatedly. *Slowly, slowly.*

We inched along because of the threat of altitude sickness, not because we lacked energy or motivation. The elevation gain from the base camp to the summit is almost 4,000 feet, posing a risk for acute illness, including high-altitude pulmonary edema. So many people make it close to the top but are forced to turn around because they become lightheaded, nauseated, short of breath, or exhibit other symptoms of altitude sickness. This is where having an experienced and informed guide makes a life-or-death difference. Everyone feels lightheaded or short of breath at 19,000 feet, but there's a need to recognize when minor symptoms edge closer to severe. Guides who fail to identify those signs or hikers who fail to listen to their guides risk grave consequences.

What a heartbreak it would be, I thought, to fly so far, to hike so far, to have to turn around at the last moment. But better close than hurt or worse. A forty-three-year-old man had to be airlifted from the top only a few hours ahead of us on the trail.

We summitted at sunset, based on the wisdom of one of our older guides who could read the clouds in the sky and saw the potential for a storm. This final push to the top required patience and concentration. We barely spoke. Because Kilimanjaro is a dormant volcano, the "top" is more of a ridge than a peak and is difficult to see. There are several false summits. We simply kept moving, stepping in one footprint after another. Slowly, slowly. The light grew dim when we made it to the top.

As the sun dipped below the horizon, we reached the sign covered in flags representing different countries. Ted wrote my mom's name on a rock and put it on one of the ledges. I loved the idea of her little stone up there, sitting on the top of the world, taking in the view.

We climbed Kilimanjaro on our tenth wedding anniversary. We married at the ocean and celebrated at the top of a mountain a decade later.

Incredibly, we found a trip itinerary that allowed the summit to be on the actual date. Ted must have mentioned this to the trek company ahead of time because one of our guides surprised us with a cake at the top. Someone made, packed, and carried this cake to and from every single campsite and all the way to the summit. The guides gathered around us in a circle, sang an African song, and danced. It is still incredible to me to think of them dancing at 19,000 feet.

We will never top that anniversary above the clouds. Photos could never capture the magic of that scene. But of everything, the stillness remains the most unforgettable part.

Be still, and know that I am God. The wind whistled, and the light darkened. I tucked my hand up into my mitten and reached for the bracelet on my wrist. On that mountain, in those quiet and uncluttered moments, I experienced God without distraction and felt my mom's presence.

The stillness and the knowing. The love and the lament.

While we were gone, over a thousand miles away, a man opened fire from a thirty-second-floor suite in the Mandalay Bay Hotel in Las Vegas, Nevada. He fired more than one thousand bullets into a crowd gathered for a country music concert. He killed sixty people and injured hundreds more—867 to be exact—a horrific tragedy. The story filled the 24-hour news cycle. We knew nothing of it until we returned to the hotel and turned on our phones and laptop computers.

This staggering news, along with a flood of texts and emails from home, barreled into my brain. I never recognized the constant buzz in my mind caused by information overload until I went a week without it. The buzz came rushing back after the break. A barrage of words and images filled the spaces that had been temporarily emptied. Real life exists at high decibels.

The stillness I found on that mountain faded when we stepped off the trail. I thought I'd never be as purely present as in those silent stretches in Africa.

Eventually, the leather on the bracelet wore down, and the imprinted words of the psalm cracked and faded. A few months later, the clasp broke after I pulled a sweater over my head. I put the bracelet in a box on a shelf, along with other items in need of repair.

Now, the broken bracelet rested among the strewed pieces on the closet floor. I knelt and reached for it and then sat back on my heels, running my fingers across the leather and the faded words. I closed my eyes. *Be still.* Breathe in. *And know.* Breathe out.

After a few rounds like this, the same sensations returned. I couldn't believe how similar and real it felt, even five years later. God without the distraction. The presence of my mom. Stillness and knowing. Love and lament. Here, in this closet.

I thought space mattered, that the mountain gave me those things, and the bracelet reminded me. But it turned out I didn't need either one. The bracelet was broken, and the mountain was an ocean away.

Because the stillness was inside of me. It had been inside of me the whole time.

Just like the words.

chapter 31

After January 21, 2022

In the days, weeks, and months following the burglary, I logged so many hours in front of a laptop screen, scanning eBay, Craigslist, Poshmark, Facebook Marketplace, and other online jewelry resale stores. Sometimes, I'd see items that looked so like mine that I'd distrust my memory, convinced these look-alikes belonged to me and I had cracked the case. But they never were mine. They always had some feature or characteristic that differentiated the doppelgängers from my missing things.

I lost whole afternoons in searches—scrolling, scrolling, scrolling—looking for a needle in a haystack while someone kept adding more piles of hay to the stack.

What if I try different search terms?

Only one more page, then I'll stop.

Click on similar items.

One more page.

Scrolling, scrolling, scrolling.

Wait, that looks like it.

No, it's not.

Okay, just ten more minutes.

I kept vigil on the local news and any reports of burglaries and thefts, and forwarded the police any semi-related media reports. Someone always knew someone who knew someone. I spoke with all the *someones* I could track down and forwarded any tidbits of information for possible leads. But the more I looked, the more I realized how often this crime happens and how long these cases remain unsolved. Everyone had a similar story, which both comforted and dispirited me.

My list of pawn shops to visit had no end. There are hundreds in the Denver metro area alone. Every time I stepped foot inside one of these stores and heard the door chimes jingle behind me, the exact same knot in my stomach tightened again.

I hate this, I thought, quickly scanning the store's hodgepodges of electronics, power tools, appliances, computers, weapons, and jewelry. I walked along the glass counters and inspected the rows of rings, bracelets, and necklaces, each piece competing for attention. My eyes darted up and down, back and forth. I willed those pieces to be mine in the same way I had when I scanned the online pages. Sometimes, I'd see what I so desperately wanted to see and ask the salesperson if I could try on a ring, confident it was mine. But as soon as I put it on my finger, I knew I was wrong.

Inside the cases, the necklaces hung on display trees, so crowded they appeared to be one mass of mixed metals. Open velvet boxes displayed the rings secured in place inside the creases. The jewelry seldom had any obvious organization, as if each new piece that joined the lot simply assumed any available open space. It reminded me of a crowded yoga class with mats overlapping and bodies squeezing together to accommodate.

I became an efficient pawn store shopper, never spending more than ninety seconds in one store because I'd learned how to recognize my jewelry in an instant. Nevertheless, it stunned me to see such gorgeous pieces with price tags at a fraction of their value. What twisted kind of fate landed them scattered among cameo pendants and gold crosses, under half-lit and blinking fluorescent lights, and only ten feet away from handguns and electric drills?

The lockets especially broke my heart. I thought of the photos that had to be removed before they could be sold, imagining tiny crumpled-up photo paper heads of loved ones tossed in the trashcan behind the counter.

I looked at so many single earrings, diamonds without their mates. One earring in one hole of a little cardboard square, the other slot empty and longing. These single earrings reminded me of those best friend necklaces from childhood—one-half of a broken heart.

Week after week, store after store, I continued my laps around the counters. But after a few months, I simply couldn't do it anymore. I had barely put a dent in a list of pawn shops in Denver alone. I wanted to believe my items never made it out of the city, when the likelihood is, as the police said, the thieves immediately shipped them out of state, maybe even out of the country. I so desperately wanted for the police to be wrong, but their theory explained why none of the leads in the case ever panned out.

The dryer repair man had an alibi. The strange unmarked white van a few people saw around the neighborhood never returned after that week. The fingerprint analysis came back inconclusive. The landscape and construction companies cried no foul play. The media reports and the stories proved to be dead ends. None of my neighbors' camera footage from that afternoon revealed anything helpful to the case.

The police moved on. Everyone moved on. The more days logged after January 21, the less everyone cared or remembered. Whatever urgency existed on that day dwindled, and life went on because life goes on. Life has no other choice but to go on.

I still held hope that something would pop up somewhere and I'd recognize it. Occasionally, I'd type "gold butterfly necklace" into the eBay search bar or scan Craigslist for "princess-cut diamond rings." Hoping for both a miracle and a really good story.

One morning, after many months of work with nothing to show for it, I decided to stop.

Nancy Drew is a young person's book heroine and Nancy Drewing (investigating without any real training) is a young person's game. I became too tired and too sad to keep going. Accepting the fact that I probably wouldn't ever see my things again, I stopped clicking and scrolling and shut my laptop. I folded up the list of pawn shops and put it in a drawer.

I walked into my office and found the list of items with descriptions that we'd made for the police and sat down at my desk, grabbed a pen and some paper, and began to write down the stories that attached to them: what ultimately became this book. I wrote the stories of the things I lost, and then I wrote the stories of the things that remained.

With time, my sense of self and my past expanded, and the heartache over the loss diminished. I had hoped to find a mystery solved, and restitution.

But in the end, I found something better.

It took a burglary for me to find a better heirloom.

There is a Bible verse in the book of Isaiah, concerning the day when God will "give a crown of beauty for ashes."

Beauty for ashes.

These pages, these stories, became a beauty for ashes trade for me. I lost my precious things, maybe, probably, forever. But in telling the stories behind them, I created something more sacred, something that can never be lost, and something that made me whole in a way the return of the pieces never could. I never would have considered the meaning and significance of those pieces if they had not been stolen and would never have had the occasion to reach out to family members or friends to revisit memories long forgotten. The stories, and the process of writing them, connected me to my past and to the people I love the most in the world, including, and maybe especially, those people I've lost.

On the night of the burglary, I prayed for peace and clarity in the confusion. I never made sense of the crime—most crimes are senseless anyway—yet I ended up making better sense of my life. I prayed for the thieves to have a change of heart, and it ended up being my own heart that changed, and for the better.

One cold Thursday morning, a few weeks after the burglary, I sat in my car in the parking lot, enjoying a few minutes of warmth before a meeting. I yanked my bag from the rear seat and opened my car door. A rush of icy air slapped me in the face. After stepping down onto the pavement, I heard a tap on the passenger side window. I ducked my head in the car and saw my friend Merritt. I fell back into my seat, closed the door, and rolled down the window.

"Can I get in here with you for a second?" she said as she opened the door and slid into the passenger seat. "I have something for you."

"What? Why?"

"Last weekend I went shopping with a friend. I found this gold necklace I loved, and so I bought it. But when I brought it home, I changed my mind. I went back yesterday to return it and buy something else, and I saw this under the glass counter."

She handed me a long rectangular box.

"Oh, my goodness. No. You didn't have to—"

"I did," she interrupted.

I opened the box and saw a dainty and very thin gold chain with a tiny charm. The letter *N* in small pavé diamonds sparkled as the light streaming in through the sunroof reflected off them.

N for *Nancy*.

I looked over at her.

"It's not the same as your mom's ring. But it's a new thing, a new reminder of her."

"No, I can't possibly. This is too much. I—"

"Yes, you can. God nudged me to do this, and I want you to have it."

"Thank you," I said, choking up. "Thank you."

She leaned over and helped clasp it around my neck. I pulled down the sun visor to look into the mirror and reached up to touch the little *N* and placed my hand over it.

"I will never forget this."

A couple of days later, another friend Kacy sent me a gift of gray pearl earrings. The note read: *To help you start your new collection.*

My friend Shannon helped replace two stolen necklaces. The necklaces had been discontinued but she reached out to a few of her connections and found some extra inventory. Barbara, my mother-in-law, brought a velvet box to the boys' basketball game a few weeks after the burglary. The box contained a beautiful silver cross necklace she had received as a gift in 1972. Aunt Jenn found another gold ring that belonged to my grandma. It fit perfectly on my right ring finger.

With these few pieces, I slowly started rebuilding what had been razed.

The generosity of family and friends helped me start to pick up the pieces, to put things back together, and to make restitution on my terms.

A couple of months after the burglary, I saw a pair of gold stud earrings on a store clearance rack. The earrings had the word *love* written in cursive with a tiny cubic zirconia stone in the *O* letter. I appreciated the daintiness of these earrings—you'd have to look closely to make out the word. But I also picked them as a reminder that I could replace what I lost with love.

Some things can never be replaced. Same with people.

But love can fill empty spaces. In a closet, and in a heart.

Antique Gold Pocket Watch

Epilogue

In Ted's office, a gold pocket watch in a shadow box frame hangs on the wall. The people who broke into our home didn't take it. No thief would think a piece of jewelry would reside on an office wall.

The watch belonged to his great-grandfather, and Ted's mom framed and gifted the watch to Ted for one of his birthdays. Because the watch is an old and interesting heirloom, it stays behind the glass and is protected in the shadow. The box has a designated place on a greige-painted wall with other framed photographs and art.

Ted loves this watch because it belonged to his great-grandfather, but he knows nothing of the man. Ted never met him, never saw a photo of him, never heard a description of his appearance or personality. He can't tell a single story of how this man's life unfolded, where he lived, or what he did for work. He isn't aware of how his mother came to possess the watch or its whereabouts when the watch stopped at exactly 10:50. Was it in his great-grandfather's pocket at the time or another person's pocket?

Ted doesn't know the story of the watch, but at least he has this beautiful antique artifact. Someday, he will give it to one of our sons with the words, *This watch belonged to your great-great grandfather*. Our son will likely hang it on a wall in his house until the time comes for it to be passed down once more, perhaps to his child. Our son will hand the box to one of our grandchildren with the words, *This watch belonged to your great-great-great grandfather.* Maybe this grandchild will hang it on a wall and maybe, one day, he or she will pass the watch on to the next generation.

But with every exchange, the watch's details will blur a little more. One day it will simply be an old watch in a shadow box frame belonging to someone in the family. The watch will hang on walls in perpetuity until someone no longer wants it on a wall. Maybe it will be set aside, in a pile with other framed items that have also outgrown their audiences. Then, maybe it will be crammed into a closet corner. Years later, it might be lost in a move, in one of the cardboard boxes that somehow never made it into the new house. Maybe the watch will be mistakenly sold at a garage sale, or a leaky pipe will flood the basement and destroy the watch. Maybe one day, someone will break into the house and steal it.

The watch's fate is uncertain, even if it is secured by a mount and protected behind glass.

Things come in and out of our possession. Sometimes by our design. Sometimes not. We can't guarantee the future of our things, and no matter how tightly we grip them, there is still going to be air between our fingers.

For a while after the burglary, I experienced real sorrow and cried honest tears. My reaction made me feel shallow and materialistic, unable to explain why I felt so devastated by this loss, why it hurt more than it should. It defied logic.

I had lived enough to experience loss. Loss made its way into my life a decade before the burglary. Three of four grandparents died over five years. Miscarriage took a pregnancy. Cancer took my mom. Suicide took a dear friend. A burglary shouldn't have packed the punch it did. Surely, I had built up enough armor by then.

And yet, I could not deny the hurt.

It might have stemmed from my guilt for being too careless and never having gotten around to installing an alarm system. Or maybe it hurt because these people violated my home, my most personal space, and stole my most coveted belongings. I could also attribute the hurt to the cumulative value of this jewelry, swept away in a matter of minutes, or maybe it was the sheer quantity of things stolen.

But there was always something else, something deeper, and I didn't recognize it until I held these pages in my hands.

When I lost things that connected me to memories of people, it felt like losing the people for the second time. When I lost things that connected me to the past, it felt like losing my history.

What made my precious things precious had nothing to do with stones or metals or value. What made them precious was what they represented, what they commemorated, and what they revealed about the human experience. My human experience.

Our artifacts might be evidence we existed. But the stories behind those artifacts are evidence we lived.

The burglars looked at my mom's ring and saw a beautiful princess-cut diamond. They did not see any of the details that happened for that ring to end up on that closet shelf. They could not know the cancer that took her away from me. On my grandma's silver wedding band, they saw tiny triangle diamonds. They did not understand what happened on the date engraved inside, a union of two immigrant families. They could not see how those coral flower earrings reminded me of a dear friend and a loss I feel every single day. On the silver fingerprint necklace, they saw a shiny disc with ridge designs. They did not recognize those ridges as the actual fingerprints of three kids and the yearning and prayers that helped usher them into the world. They knew nothing of my boundless love for them.

Sometimes stuff is just stuff. Sometimes stuff is more.

When I lost these keepsakes, I believed I also lost what and who they represented, as if my memories had been fused into the metals, woven into the chains, etched into the stones. This loss compounded all my other losses and untethered me from my past.

But the stories brought me back.

And no one can ever steal the stories.

author's note

As I write these words, concluding this project that has meant so much to me, it is impossible to ignore the devastating fires still raging in California. We are only beginning to understand the extent of the damage and loss. Now the slow process begins of picking up the pieces and rebuilding something new. This tragedy came on the heels of hurricanes that ravaged North Carolina and other parts of the southeastern United States in late 2024, wind and rain destroying lives and other precious things. For anyone who may have experienced the heartbreak that accompanies the loss of valuable and invaluable items, either in these fires, hurricanes, or other harrowing events, my heart goes out to you. It is my wish that this book can provide a template to navigate such an unexpected and hurtful forfeiture and maybe, hopefully, allow you to make a beauty for ashes trade.

Please share your stories with me at
www.kimdanielson.com.

KD
January 2025

discussion questions

1. Did reading this book change your perspective on material possessions? Why or why not?

2. Was there any one line that stood out to you?

3. How did the author explore topics such as identity, family, relationships, spirituality, or legacy?

4. Which piece of jewelry in the book resonated the most with you? Why?

5. Have you ever lost something important to you? What happened? What emotions did you feel in the wake of this loss?

6. Pick your most treasured material object/possession. Describe the circumstances around receiving it and what it represents to you.

7. What do you think is the biggest takeaway from the book?

sources & notes

Chapter 2

Gemological Institute of America. "Topaz." www.gia.edu/topaz.

Knuth, Bruce G. *Gems in Myth, Legend and Lore*. Parachute, CO: Jewelers Press, 2007.

Sinclair, H. R. *A Writer's Guide to Crystals and Gemstones*. Independently published, 2023. Ebook.

Chapter 4

Merriam-Webster.com Dictionary. "Heirloom." www.merriam-webster.com/dictionary/heirloom.

Chapter 6

Academy of Natural Sciences of Drexel University. "Butterfly Life Cycle." www.ansp.org/exhibits/online-exhibits/butterflies/lifecycle/.

American Museum of Natural History. "Butterfly Metamorphosis." www.amnh.org/exhibitions/butterflies/metamorphosis.

Chapter 8

Gemological Institute of America. "The History of the Engagement Ring." www. 4cs.gia.edu/en-us/blog/istory-engagement-ring/.

Raden, Aja. *Stoned: Jewelry, Obsession, and How Desire Shapes the World*. New York: Ecco, 2015.

With These Rings Handmade. "History of Wedding Rings." wwww.withtheseringshandmade.com/history-of-wedding-rings.

Chapter 10

Brown, T. S. "The History Behind Poesy Rings." www.tsbrown.com/pages/the-history-behind-poesy-rings.

Chapter 12

American Gem Society. "Sapphire History." www.americangemsociety.org/birthstones/september-birthstone/sapphire-history/.

Gemological Institute of America. "Sapphire: History and Lore." www.gia.edu/sapphire-history-lore.

Simmons, Robert and Naisha Ahsian. *The Book of Stones: Who They Are and What They Teach*. Rochester, VT: Inner Traditions, 2005.

Sinclair, H.R. *A Writer's Guide to Crystals and Gemstones.*

Chapter 14

Psalm 42:7 (ESV). Scripture quotations marked (ESV) are from The ESV® Bible (The Holy Bible, English Standard Version®), © 2001 by Crossway, a publishing ministry of Good News Publishers. Used by permission. All rights reserved.

Chapter 16

VanVoorst, Jenny Fretland. *Gems*. Minneapolis, MN: Abdo Publishing, 2015.

Chapter 18

Butcher, Amanda. "History of Birthstones." *International Gem Society*. www.gemsociety.org/article/history-of-birthstones/.

Pearl, Richard M. *Popular Gemology*. Read Books, 2016. Ebook.

Simmons and Ahsian, *The Book of Stones.*

Chapter 20

Editors of Encyclopedia Britannica. "Criminal Investigation." *Encyclopedia Britannica*. www.britannica.com/topic/criminal-investigation.

Editors of Encyclopedia Britannica. "Fingerprint." *Encyclopedia Britannica*. www.britannica.com/topic/fingerprint.

Kaushal, Nitan, and Purnima Kaushal. "Human Identification and Fingerprints: A Review." *Journal of Biometrics and Biostatistics*. www.brainscanthailand.com/wp-content/uploads/2018/10/human-identification-and-fingerprints-a-review-2155-6180.1000123.pdf.

Chapter 22

Editors of Encyclopedia Britannica. "Millefiori Glass." *Encyclopedia Britannica*. www.britannica.com/art/millefiori-glass.

Chapter 24

Crowe, Judith. *Jeweler's Directory of Gemstones*. Richmond Hill, ON: Firefly Books, 2012.

Etymonline. "Diamond." www.etymonline.com/search?q=diamond.

Gemological Institute of America. "The Origin of Wedding Rings: Ancient Tradition or Marketing Invention?" www.4cs.gia.edu/en-us/blog/origin-of-wedding-rings/.

Simmons and Ahsian, *The Book of Stones*.

Chapter 26

LeGrand, Douglas S. "Early History of Jewelry: Ancient Times to the 17th Century." *International Gem Society*. www.gemsociety.org/article/ myth-magic-and-the-sorcerers-stone/.

Merriam-Webster.com Dictionary. "Chain." www.merriam-webster.com/dictionary/chain.

Chapter 28

Beecher, Rev. Luther F. "The Parable of Immortality." 1904. In the public domain. Also attributed to Henry Van Dyke.

Color Meanings. "Coral Color Meaning: The Color Coral." www.color-meanings.com/coral-color-meaning-the-color-coral/.

Chapter 30

Psalm 46:10 (ESV).

Chapter 31

Isaiah 61:3 (NLT). Scripture quotations marked (NLT) are taken from the Holy Bible, New Living Translation, copyright ©1996, 2004, 2015 by Tyndale House Foundation. Used by permission of Tyndale House Publishers, Carol Stream, Illinois 60188. All rights reserved.

acknowledgments

Truly, this book would not exist without four extraordinary writers whom I am honored to call my friends. Denise Brandt, Cheryl Rodeheffer, Ann Spence, and Stephanie Webb—you helped turn a caterpillar into a butterfly. Thank you for your many reads and edits, sage advice, and endless encouragement. Ours is one of those circles that lasts.

Thank you to the entire *Book Incubator* team, including Mary Adkins, Joselin Linder, Rufi Thorpe, Harrison Gale, Liz Pickart, Gayle Brown, Lucas Schaefer, Ashley Strosnider, and Emma Dries. Your individual and collective wisdom helped me resist giving up on myself. Keep making writers' dreams come true.

Many thanks to everyone at *She Writes Press*, especially Brooke Warner and Addison Gallegos, for bringing a Word document to actual life. There's no better gift anyone could give an author than a belief in her work. You're blazing such an important trail, and I'm happy to be under your banner.

I'd like to express my gratitude to the incredible editors who helped this book become the best version of itself. Finn Ruehrdanz and Rachel Lehmann-Haupt, your brilliance, time, and thoughtfulness made all the difference.

I want to thank my first readers, Julie Edge, Ursula Stuter, and Maya Weiss. It's a terrifying thing to give your words over to someone else, and you handled an early draft with care and gentleness. Maya, I want you to know I'm so proud of you. To my first-ever writing pal, Angelo Mancino, you are an absolute gem.

Thank you to Jared Hankins not only for your incredible artist mind but also for your patience and long-suffering kindness in this process. Fatikhun Najib, your remarkable talent and vision made this book complete.

I want to thank Caitlin Hamilton Summie for envisioning a bright future for this book and creative ways to get there.

I have many friends to thank, those mentioned on these pages, as well as others who have shown up for me in big and small ways, though they've all been big to me. I am especially grateful to Christina Alexiades, Tina Cotton, Dawn Fable, Gayle Lessmann, Emily Macht, and Mandy Sandhaus. Writing a book is such a solitary endeavor, but for a writer, it means everything when someone asks, "What's going on with your book?" These women asked, and often. Thanks for being my cheerleaders. You are pearls on my strand.

To Aunt Jenn, thank you for reading this book on your phone within minutes of receiving an early draft. Thanks also for always being there for me.

To Dad, Nick, and Adam, we share so many of these memories. I wouldn't be who I am without you.

To Mom, Lindsay, and my grandparents, I hope I've honored you here. Until I see you on the shoreline, I'll be missing you on this side.

To Ted, thank you for supporting me and this dream, and for understanding when it didn't make sense. I love you.

To my boys, Calvin, Cooper, and Crosby, thank you for announcing in your classes and to your friends that your mom was a published author long, long before she became one. You know, none of this means a thing without the three of you.

about the author

Photo credit to Gayle Lessmann

Kim Danielson practiced law on both ends of the spectrum, first as a public defender and then as a corporate attorney. In 2019, she founded a nonprofit organization to support teachers impacted by cancer. In all her work, she has witnessed countless examples of goodness stemming from loss, and this kind of restoration is a major undercurrent in her writing and life. She lives in Denver with her husband and three sons.

Looking for your next great read?

We can help!

Visit www.shewritespress.com/next-read
or scan the QR code below for a list
of our recommended titles.